D0429509

DATE DUE

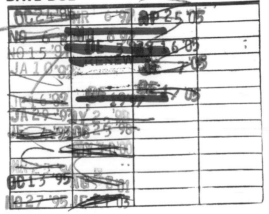

HAWTHORNE'S
SECRET

Hawthorne's Secret

AN UN-TOLD TALE

Philip Young

David R. Godine · *Publisher* · BOSTON

First published in 1984 by
David R. Godine, Publisher, Inc.
306 Dartmouth Street
Boston, Massachusetts 02116

LIBRARY OF CONGRESS CATALOGING IN PUBLICATION DATA

Young, Philip, 1918-
    Hawthorne's secret.

    1. Hawthorne, Nathaniel, 1804-1864. 2. Novelists,
American—19th century—Biography. I. Title.
PS1881.Y58 1984   813'.3 [B]   83-48891
    ISBN 0-87923-515-2

First edition

Printed in the United States of America

This book is inscribed to
RICHARD E. WINSLOW III
who has traveled a good deal in Salem

Let not the reader argue . . . that the times of
the Puritans were more vicious than our own,
when . . . we discern no badge of infamy on
man or woman. It was the policy of our ancestors to search out even the most secret sins,
and expose them. . . . Were such the custom
now, perchance we might find materials for a
no less piquant sketch.

"Endicott and the Red Cross,"
Hawthorne, 1838

CONTENTS

INTRODUCTION

The Custom-House Mysteries

Ｏｎ a fine day the building sparkles, red and white against the blue. Crested by a great gold eagle perching over the sign that says CUSTOM HOUSE, it is a tourist shrine. The faithful file through, occasionally asking to see the place where, according to his story, Nathaniel Hawthorne, on a rainy day long ago, poked into some heaped-up rubbish and uncovered a mysterious package of aged documents and an old piece of red cloth in the shape of an *A*. The wharves out front were already crumbling then, but the building was unfinished. He describes its second floor, where he says he came upon the artifacts, as a large, shabby attic. Now that custom is no longer housed there, tidy rooms occupy the area. The scene of the find is erased.

But not from the national memory, where it has lurked for 130 years. Countless souls who have never visited Salem, Massachusetts, have toured "The Custom-House" introduction to *The Scarlet Letter*. It has been explored in many thousands of classrooms, and by many scholars. Thus it is hard to explain why two striking mysteries in the familiar entrance to America's classic romance should have been virtually ignored.

The first concerns the confession with which the author opens his book. Not that confession is out of order. In the end, that is what the book urges. "Be true!" Hawthorne cries at the close. "Show freely to the world, if not your worst, yet some trait whereby the worst may be inferred!" The odd thing is what at the start he confesses himself: his inheritance of the guilt of his Salem ancestors.

How did he share in it? He says that the "grave, bearded . . . progenitor" of American Hawthornes, "who came so early with his Bible and his sword," was possessed of "all the Puritan traits, both good and evil." He was "a bitter persecutor; as witness the Quakers, who have remembered him in their histories." This man's son, the author continues, "inherited the persecuting spirit, and made himself so conspicuous in the martyrdom of the witches, that their blood may fairly be said to have left a stain upon him." Whether or not these men repented their sins, Hawthorne continues, "I, the present writer . . . hereby take shame upon myself for their sakes, and pray that any curse incurred by them"—he has heard of one—"be now and henceforth removed." All very well perhaps. What is curious is the admission that comes out of this: "Strong traits of their nature have intertwined themselves with mine."

How so? The explanation that this refers to a "coolness" in the way Hawthorne "studied" people is lame and feeble. In the great deal that is known of his life and character, the persecuting spirit is nowhere visible. "He loves power," remarked his wife, "as little as any mortal I ever knew." The strong traits of their nature have never been found in his.

Given the depths of his book, the second confession is equally peculiar. This is that his story had a profounder meaning than the writer managed to convey in composing it. Having told the tale, he had not "fathomed its deeper import. A better book than I shall ever write was there." Similarly with the red letter. It was a "mystic symbol," which kept "evading the analysis of my mind." No one has determined what depth of his symbol escaped him, or what better book lay deeper in its matter. Hence no one has suggested that it was a darker one. Or that its darkness might connect with the unexplained confession of inherited ancestral guilt.

Even Longfellow, long a friend, judged Hawthorne "a mysterious man." Shortly after her husband died, Mrs. Hawthorne remarked, "The sacred veil of his eyelids he scarcely lifted to himself. . . . Such an unviolated sanctuary was his nature, I his inmost wife, never conceived or knew." The "veil he drew around him," she added, should not be lifted. No one has succeeded in lifting it. The notion that he had something to hide has been discredited for decades—buried under heaped-up biographical data. Long on information, short in understanding, lives of Hawthorne accumulate endlessly. The notion that there *was* some secret has long appeared hopelessly romantic, culturally lagged, an embarrassment to the well informed. These people, on the other hand, are forced to believe that a writer preoccupied with sin and guilt, whose insight into these matters has "perhaps never been surpassed," had no deep experience of them. After he died, his sister Elizabeth remarked to his son, Julian, "Your father kept his very existence a secret, as far as possible." It is hard to think that a man could have gone to his grave with a burden on his conscience, and perhaps in his books, which over a century of steady scrutiny has failed to uncover. Yet the most powerful and penetrating mind and spirit that ever came up against Hawthorne's believed it. Julian said Herman Melville told him "there was some secret in my father's life which has never been revealed." Nor did Melville think it a trivial one: it "accounted for the gloomy passages in his books." This was the man who wrote that the "great power of blackness" was at the heart of Hawthorne's genius.

Confidence in Melville's intuition, if that was the source of his suspicion about a secret, is generally high. More suggestive still, however, is the realization that some of those best informed on Hawthorne, such as his most recent and thorough biographers, are either unaware of extraordinary facts that relate directly to matters he kept secret, or have silently and completely suppressed them (to protect their subject from possible disrepute, presumably). As for his critics, even the best have not gone so far as they might into areas that contain anxieties which preoccupied him early and late. The vast majority of his readers, as a result, are insensible of an enormous gap in their knowledge of the family past he immersed himself in, made his own, and attempted to put to use in several failed romances as well as two successful ones.

In this study, a short account of Hawthorne's life and a selective survey of his work are calculated to point in the direction of aspects of the record that have gone unexplained or unremarked. A longer section then attempts to throw light back on the literature and its author. What is revealed in the end is a son of his forefathers who had at least some reason to believe he had inherited a "moral disease" or "bad passion"—a phenomenon *The House of the Seven Gables* set out to describe. Once the facts of this ancestral curse become clear, so does the nature of his own guilty secret. There was a lot more to it than Melville could ever in the world have known.

ONE

"If Ever I Should Have a Biographer ..."

JULIAN Hawthorne is patron saint of all who
reject Melville's suspicion that Hawthorne
had a significant secret. Himself an early biographer, Julian argued that his father "had no
stain . . . upon his conscience. . . . The closet . . .
had no skeleton in it; there was nothing to be
hidden." He particularly objected to the con-
struction of an imaginary Hawthorne from his
work. Very well, one begins with his life, of
which the work was a large part.

A regional son of New England, with little
or no feeling for the country as a whole, it is
faintly ironic that Hawthorne was born, in 1804,
on the Fourth of July. In a sense he was a son of
Salem. His roots there were deep. On his mother's
side he was a Manning, a clan that traced back
to a captain, Nicholas, who arrived there in 1662
and eventually made a name for himself. Until
Nathaniel did too, Manning was a name more
prominent in Salem than Hawthorne, though
the writer never mentioned a Manning directly

in his work. The forebears he wrote about are remembered. Their progenitor was William Ha-thorne (1607–1681), a major and a magistrate who may have arrived here as early as 1630. Couples whose firstborn appeared too soon after marriage appeared before him. So did a woman of Boston who was sentenced to sit on a stool in the marketplace with a sign at her bosom that read THUS I STAND FOR MY ADULTEROUS AND WHORISH CARRIAGE. What the Quakers recalled was the shy young wife of Salem who was sentenced to be stripped to the waist, tied to the tail of a cart, and whipped to her house. The major's "good Puritan trait," in Nathaniel's eyes, would have been disobedience of an order of Charles II to return to England in 1666. William's son John (1641–1717) was not quite the "witch judge" the author called him. Nor any judge on whom a condemned witch pro-nounced the curse, "God will give you blood to drink!" These were family traditions, still believed in Julian's day, but John too was a magistrate, who helped determine which sus-pects the judges should try as witches. He wit-nessed the executions, and was present when Sarah Good placed the famous curse on the minister Nicholas Noyes.

Descended from yeomen of Hawthorn Hill, Berkshire, all the American Hawthornes down to the writer, who restored the *w* to the name, had titles of command which would never have suited the Hawthorne best remembered. Major Hathorne's son John was a colonel, and his son Joseph was a sea captain. So was his son Daniel, a patriot privateersman of the American Revolution, subject of a ballad, "Bold Hathorne." A sea captain in turn was Nathaniel, father of the author, who married, on August 1, 1801, the black-haired, gray-eyed beauty Elizabeth Clarke Manning. After four months he took sail and returned in the spring of 1803 to meet his black-haired, gray-eyed daughter, Elizabeth Manning Hathorne, born seven months and five days after the wedding. At the end of the year he sailed again, and returned to greet Nathaniel, Junior, four months. He never saw his second daughter, Mary Louisa. When she was three months old— Elizabeth was six and Nathaniel almost four— her mother called the older children into her room, looked at the boy, and said, "Your father is dead." In the Dutch colony of Surinam, he was carried off by yellow fever.

Elizabeth remembered the scene a generation after her brother died. Called Ebe after the sound he made as a baby attempting her name, she was the family star. According to tradition, she could walk, talk, and understand all that was said to her at the age of nine months. When they were schoolgirls, Elizabeth Peabody, future educator, pronounced her "brilliant"—"a genius." Her brother was handsome and sturdy. But with the father's death the family suffered financial emergency and instant obscurity. Not far from destitute, the widow moved almost next door—back into the Manning house on Herbert Street she had left for so short a time. At the Mannings' the Hawthorne females lived in one room; the boy shared with his Uncle Robert a "chamber under the eaves" directly over it. The reclusiveness of his mother, challenged by apologists for the family, was in fact stunning. Nathaniel declared as a grown man she "has never sat down to table with anybody, since my father's death." Before he could recall her dining with him, he was well into middle age. For forty years she wore the clothes the young wife had owned, and almost never left her room. Elizabeth Peabody remembered a rare appearance. With the lovely face and ancient costume, she "looked as if she had walked out of an old picture."

The temporary loss, at nine, of the use of a foot is the other best-known fact of her son's boyhood. For two years the injury resisted even the therapy in which he stuck it out a window while water was poured on it from a window above. But it granted freedom from school—to loaf and to read. After a cure by Dr. Time, as

Ebe put it, she and her brother became—as they remained—great walkers. They also read all they could, the boy taking on Spenser, Bunyan, Shakespeare, Boswell's Johnson, almost all of Scott's fiction, and, in translation, Rousseau's *Nouvelle Héloïse* ("Admirable," he thought). Elizabeth was beautiful like her mother; even in adolescence she was reclusive, independent, and formidable. As a grown man Hawthorne would say, "I fear nothing in life so much as Ebe's ridicule." Their sister Louisa was friendly, girlish, and no threat.

Another release was the summertime removal of the family to Raymond, Maine, where the Mannings owned land on Sebago Lake. The boy loved the woods and water, hunting and fishing. But in spite of all intentions and even resolutions, Ebe remarked, "By some fatality we all seemed to be brought back to Salem." For her brother this meant chiefly to Uncle Robert—a substitute father if a boy ever had one—under whose eye he struggled to achieve a degree of independence. As it happened, Robert Manning was a pomologist of international repute, said to have had the largest orchards—including a thousand varieties of pears alone—in America. Manning made plans for the boy, who kept plans to himself. But against his wishes, Nathaniel was very frequently separated from his immediate family, shuttling between Raymond and Salem. In 1821 Robert decided he should attend Bowdoin College. He was prepared for admission, and wrote business letters at the Manning office. The Mannings owned the stagecoach line to Boston, established by Nathaniel's grandfather, originally a blacksmith. The boy was agreeable to Bowdoin partly because he expected to vacation from it with his family—who had been returned to Salem. When he was in Salem, his mother and the girls were at Raymond. On one occasion he met up with a striking young woman, and at first failed to recognize his sister Ebe.

College began without enthusiasm, ended without distinction. "I was an idle student," Hawthorne wrote, "negligent of college rules." He ranked eighteenth, at graduation, out of thirty-eight. He was friend or acquaintance of fellow students of future note: an American President, Franklin Pierce, the American poet, Longfellow, and Horatio Bridge—lawyer, businessman, and naval officer, who was probably first to claim real literary merit for a friend who was lagging far behind his rising classmates. Nathaniel paid a remarkable number of fines for failure to attend class and church, for a stubborn refusal to declaim, and for drinking and gaming at cards. This prompted a stern letter from Ebe. He replied that moral advice from her was strange.

Bowdoin for Hawthorne was a pleasant experience. But in his senior year, looking ahead, he made a bet that is both curious and as yet unexplained. After a friendly discussion of marriage, he drafted and signed a document pledging that if on that day—November 14, 1824—twelve years hence he were "a married man or a widower . . . I bind myself . . . to pay Jonathan Cilley a barrel of the best old Madeira wine." Cilley, to whom he was closest in college, bound himself in contrary fashion. The document was left in the keeping of Bridge, his closest friend afterward. Likely this related to a plan made by a boy of seventeen who wrote his mother, "What do you think of my becoming an author?" In college he had already begun to write—perhaps a novel and very possibly some of what became in his mind "Seven Tales of My Native Land." At any rate, choice of a difficult profession makes some sense of the wager.

And of an ensuing decision. On graduation from college into what was supposed to be the real world, Hawthorne determined neither to live in it and seek his fortune like his friends, nor to go into business with the Mannings, but to disappear into his Salem chamber under the eaves, a room that would haunt him the rest of his life. Uncle Robert had married and departed the house on Herbert Street, where Mrs. Hathorne and her daughters still lived in the single state they would never relinquish. As if the place had swallowed him, son and brother lived in his old room for the next twelve years. His "natural tendency . . . toward seclusion," he wrote, "I now indulged to the utmost, so that, for months together, I scarcely held human intercourse outside my own family; seldom going out except at twilight, or only to take the nearest way to the most convenient solitude, which was oftenest the seashore." As for Salem, "I doubt whether so many as twenty people in the town were aware of my existence." As for the room, he wrote later, it

> deserves to be called a haunted chamber, for thousands upon thousands of visions have appeared to me in it; and some few of them have become visible to the world. If ever I should have a biographer, he ought to make great mention of this chamber in my memoirs, because so much of my lonely youth was wasted here, and here my mind and character were formed.

It is not clear whether he intended irony, hope, or prophecy, but late in 1836 he would write, "In this dismal and squalid chamber FAME was won." (His widow would one day strike "squalid," which to be sure is not completely

understood.) The whole period of twelve years
is not yet entirely understood. One biographer
found it "too mysterious . . . too obscure to be
altogether credible." He concluded that the
young man was a secret government agent. Much
energy has been expended to correct the author's
sketch of his solitary years. Essentially if artfully
he wrote the truth himself.

Confinement was occasionally broken with
modest trips, chiefly to other parts of New
England. Back in the room he did a lot of reading. He read many novels, and there is record of
some twelve hundred nonfiction titles that Ebe
withdrew for him from the Salem Athenaeum.
Particularly he read history—especially New
England, Massachusetts, or Salem history. By the
time he left Herbert Street, moreover, he had
written at least forty-four tales and sketches plus
a book-length fiction of his own. Some of his
work was of course abortive. He so regretted
having published *Fanshawe*, 1828—anonymously
and with his own one hundred dollars—that he
destroyed every copy he could lay hands on and
instructed others to do the same. At about the
same time, when "Seven Tales of My Native
Land" found no publisher, he burned most of
them. Neither of two other collections, "Provincial Tales" or "The Story Teller," ever appeared. Such tales and sketches as were printed

in magazines or gift books were anonymous or pseudonymous. He was, as he claimed, "for a good many years, the obscurest man of letters in America." At last in 1837 he began to emerge from the gloom with *Twice-Told Tales* under his own name. He had still not completely landed a publisher on his own, for unknown to him his friend Bridge had pledged two hundred dollars against such losses as might be incurred. There were none, but Hawthorne's own means remained meager, his future uncertain. Grandfather Manning had left him little more than fourteen hundred dollars, which produced small income. Nine pieces contributed in 1837 to *The Token* had fetched one hundred eight dollars. His two volumes for children, called *Peter Parley's Universal History* (also 1837), were still selling thirty years later. He offered the hundred dollars he got for them to Ebe for her help. For poor wages, he had previously edited—that is to say, with the same help, largely written—*The American Magazine of Useful and Entertaining Knowledge*.

For the most part Hawthorne does not appear to have been unhappy during his long retreat from the world. He did write Longfellow that he inhabited a "dungeon" in which "by some witchcraft or other" he had locked himself. And at least for a time he must have been depressed.

Fear for his fate may have been behind Bridge's
having underwritten his one acknowledged book.
In response to a disturbing letter, Bridge wrote
him in October of 1836 that he was "too good
a subject" for suicide. Another upset came two
years later, when Jonathan Cilley of the Bowdoin
wager, by then a congressman in Washington,
was killed in a duel, which shocked the country
and the writer. No one has convincingly explained why Hawthorne should have felt responsibility for Cilley's death in a political
quarrel. But ever since Julian, in his biography,
saw it as the source of his father's "guilt," the
notion has had currency. The fact is that the most
remorseful of his works, called "The Haunted
Mind," was published three years before Cilley
died—a year after Bridge was most worried about
his condition. "Fancy's Show Box," related to
it, and perhaps his most direct discussion of
guilt, appeared a year before the duel.

It was once explained that Cilley got in the
fight that determined his fate while purchasing
a barrel of Madeira. This cannot have been, but
he had lost his bet. On learning this from Bridge,
and of the forthcoming *Twice-Told Tales*
(*Twice-told*, as it appeared in Hawthorne's day),
Cilley responded with an equation of which
something might be made. He cheerfully con-
gratulated his friend on the book. But he also

remarked that he had rather have heard that Hawthorne was about to be "the author of a legitimate and well-begotten boy." He was invoking an old set of alternatives. Shakespeare in his sonnets poses, as separate paths to immortality, marriage and the generation of children, or the creation of beauty in poetry. So had Hawthorne in *Fanshawe*, which is said to lack "a controlling idea." That is because it has not been seen as an explanation of his wager and withdrawal. The idea that controls its tame story is the one Cilley expressed in his letter—book or boy. And the answer is clear for young Fanshawe: book. A later age would call this sublimation.

In Fanshawe the student Hawthorne projected his first published and far-reaching persona: the fledgling artist as lonely college boy who renounces marriage for his private vision. This is an "inmost . . . dream of undying fame . . . more powerful than a thousand realities." The portrait is of a poet—Fanshawthorne?—in standard romantic form: pale, melancholy, early blighted. He is drawn to the pretty Ellen who, to connect him to the world, generously offers her hand. This he refuses, but not because he is going to die young. The "idea" becomes clear when she marries instead the handsome and "manly" Walcott—"the poet of his class," who for his bride rejects a literary career and "the worldly dis-

tinction of which she thus deprived him." Wife
or fame. Obviously it did not seem to Fanshawe
that he could have both.

Even before he was Fanshawe, however, Hawthorne had begun to conceive a more individual
and durable mask, which he called Oberon. That
is how he signed letters to Bridge after they left
college, and while still at Bowdoin he had inscribed his commencement program Nathaniel
Oberon Hathorne. Invoking the King of the
Fairies and things generally unworldly, it was a
good name for a prospective author of "romance"
—a genre distinct in Hawthorne's mind from the
"novel," which was tied to reality. Both Oberon
and Fanshawe owed something to a tubercular
and excessively studious classmate named Deane,
who died on the eve of graduation, but they are
essentially Hawthorne as he chose to imagine
and present himself in the role of an obscure
young writer.

In "Fragments of the Journal of a Solitary
Man" (1837) Oberon has perished like Deane.
What his journal posthumously discloses is chiefly his uneasiness over the lonely course he has
set himself. He has exchanged "a young man's
bliss" in marriage for "a thousand vagrant fantasies." Even more directly autobiographical had
been "The Devil in Manuscript" (1835), where
Oberon in his quarters, reenacting the author's

own despair, burns his unpublishable tales. He is bitter about them. Not only have they led him from the beaten path of the world, they contain a "fiend." Perishing in their publication by flames, they set the town on fire. The nameless narrator of other sketches published out of Herbert Street —lonely, hidden, fantasizing observer—is precisely the same figure. In "The Village Uncle" he has been redeemed by the "domestic fire" of a woman. In "The Ambitious Guest" his "high and abstracted ambition," which was Fanshawe's —to avoid being forgotten in the grave—goes to the grave with him. In "Sights from a Steeple" he longs to hover invisibly around men and women and houses where "guilt is entering into hearts—guilt is on the very verge of commission . . . guilt is done."

In "The Haunted Mind" (1835) unnamed Oberon lies abed in the squalid chamber of such a house. Here guilt has been done, and has entered his heart. Out of its "dungeon," Passion and Feeling assume bodily shape, and in "a sort of conscious sleep" the narrator suffers his guilt in a "nightmare of the soul." Suddenly it is hard to distinguish the dungeon of his heart from the dungeon Hawthorne called his room on Herbert Street. Similarly, his haunted mind turns out to be the same place as the "haunted chamber" where the author said his mind and character were formed, where "visions" had appeared to him, some of which he had made "visible to the world." Out of "the brotherhood of remorse" three of them are revealed here. Gliding by his bed passes a "pale young mourner, wearing a sister's likeness to first love, sadly beautiful." Then the shade of a girl full of reproach. Last a demon, pointing a finger at the sore place in the young man's bosom. "What," he asks himself, "if the fiend should come in women's garments, with a pale beauty . . . and lie down by your side? What if she should stand at your bed's foot" in a bloodstained shroud? Then, starting upright, he daydreams of a "tenderer bosom," a "purer heart," beside him. He has a vision of her in a setting of flowers, an Edenic bride.

Two years later in "Fancy's Show Box" the writer starts abruptly by asking,

> What is Guilt? A stain upon the soul. And it is a point of vast interest whether the soul may contract such stains . . . from deeds which may have been plotted and resolved upon, but which, physically, have never had existence. . . . In the solitude of a midnight chamber . . . the soul may pollute itself even with those crimes which we are accustomed to deem altogether carnal.

Will these "draw the full weight of a condemning sentence"? Finally no. "The dreadful consequences of sin will not be incurred, unless the act have set its seal upon the thought." And yet though "man's hand be clean, his heart has surely been polluted. . . . Penitence must kneel." These are remarkable entries in a spiritual diary.

What they don't suggest—and nothing else we know will account for it either—is that by 1835 fictions far superior to these tentative apprentice works had already seen print. Indeed by 1829 Hawthorne had written out of the same chamber the "Provincial Tales" he was unable to publish as a volume. Among these were "My Kinsman, Major Molineux," "Roger Malvin's Burial," and "Young Goodman Brown"—which is to call attention to a fact seldom recognized: that Hawthorne wrote fiction of such maturity, power, depth, complexity, and mythic resonance as he would never surpass, and only once, in *The Scarlet Letter*, equal, before he was twenty-six.

Nor do the Oberon chapters contain any equivalent of the strange story called "Alice Doane's Appeal," which in an earlier version had survived the fires that consumed most of the other Tales of Hawthorne's Native Land. Also published in 1835, it is the rather primitive tale of a young man and his sister, Leonard and Alice Doane. Leonard is characterized by morbid feelings; there is a "deep taint" to his nature. He is maddened by a "distempered jealousy" of a "secret sympathy" between Alice and Walter

Brome, Leonard's "very counterpart." Counterpart indeed, Walter is Leonard's unknown twin, his sister's brother. An operating wizard, first of several in Hawthorne, had "cunningly devised that Walter should tempt his unknown sister to guilt and shame." Out of his jealousy, Leonard murders his twin. At the end, as if the writer had lost his nerve, Alice is absolved of the shame of which there had been "indubitable proofs." (But Leonard is not.) Hawthorne published the tale anonymously, having added a frame to the original story, and never collected it or mentioned it again. It was lost until, long after his death, an elderly lady, Ebe, remembered it clearly. A search of old magazines exhumed it. Her brother apparently chose to bury it, but she thought it possessed his "peculiar genius."

Hawthorne was exhumed with the appearance of *Twice-Told Tales,* which reprinted some trifles while including none of the extraordinary stories he had published. It was publicized with a generous review signed by the famous Longfellow, who said a new star had risen in the heavens. Elizabeth Peabody, by now well known to Boston intellectuals and living five blocks from Herbert Street, had been of the opinion that Ebe had written some of the fiction attributed to her brother. But on receiving a copy of the book from the man who wrote it, she invited him and his sisters to call one evening at the Peabodys'.

When they arrived, her sister Sophia, indisposed as commonly, was in her room. Elizabeth rushed upstairs to bring her down. "You never saw anything so splendid," she cried. "He is handsomer than Lord Byron!"

Perhaps he was, but Sophia stayed put. She was twenty-eight years old, and since girlhood at least half an invalid. She was "refined, cultivated," and, according to her son Julian, could read Latin, Greek, and Hebrew. She was excitable, intensely feminine, and afflicted with chronic, crippling headaches. Emerson admired her paintings—she was an excellent copyist—and pronounced her "fair." She was welcome as his guest at Concord, and once pronounced him "the greatest man that ever lived." When she did meet Hawthorne she felt such power that she was "alarmed," and wondered what it meant. At the sight of her he was transfixed, and soon began thinking in terms of angels. But the progress of their affair was slow.

It was impeded by Sophia's health. Since she was seventeen it had been impressed on her that she was unsuited for marriage, and she herself believed she should not inflict the care of an invalid on a husband. She was indeed fair—hair golden or chestnut brown, eyes gray-blue. Two years on a Cuban plantation with her sister Mary (later Mrs. Horace Mann) had not improved her condition. On the Hawthorne side it was argued that Nathaniel should not marry lest the shock be more than his mother could handle. Julian was almost surely right in thinking this an invention of his Aunt Ebe in her "wicked" opposition to the betrothal. "He will never marry," she announced. As Julian says, she was "resolved to do what she could to prevent it." She intercepted and appropriated a bouquet the Peabody girls sent him, explaining that he disliked flowers. Sophia was too weak to "fulfill the duties of married life." On meeting Ebe, Sophia "all at once fell in love with her. . . . Her eyes are very beautiful." She thought "extreme sensibility" made her a "hermitress." Ebe did not melt. The "mingling of another mind" would "spoil the flower" of Nathaniel's genius.

The engagement was a protracted secret. And much of the courtship was conducted by mail, Hawthorne having found employment, early in 1839, at the Boston Custom House. In the spring he moved from there, having invested his savings in "Mr. Ripley's Utopia" at Brook Farm. The idea was that communal living which combined manual and intellectual labor might agreeably support a wife and a literary career. It evaporated with the discovery that a day in the fields incapacitated one for fictions. Since his emergence into the world, indeed, he had written almost nothing but letters to his fiancée. "It is a miracle worthy even of thee," he wrote, "to have converted a life of shadows into the deepest truth, by thy magic touch." He beseeched her not to allow mesmerism to be exercised on her for the headaches. He washed his hands before reading her letters. (After they married he burned them, "hundreds of them. . . . There are no more such.") The wedding, proposed for the groom's thirty-eighth birthday, was postponed five days by an incapacitated bride of thirty-three. It took place at the Peabody house in Boston with no Hawthorne present but Nathaniel.

Even he had feared Sophia was "too delicate and exquisitely wrought . . . to dwell in this world." Predictably, it was untrue. Margaret Fuller, known to Brook Farm and Hawthorne, forecast success. "If I ever saw a man," she wrote the bride, "who combined delicate tenderness to understand the heart of a woman, with quiet depth and manliness enough to satisfy her, it is Mr. Hawthorne." So he was. If Mrs. Hawthorne drew him from the shadows, he rescued her from a sickbed. There were lapses into "nervous debility," but she joined him in the happiest marriage, very likely, enjoyed by any major American writer. They moved into the Old Manse at Concord, built by Emerson's grandfather, who watched the start of the American Revolution from one of its windows. But for them the place was Eden. The daydream of a "Haunted Mind" was realized. "Oh lovely God!" wrote Sophia in her journal,

> I thank thee that I can rush into my sweet husband with all my many waters, & sing & thunder with all my waves in the vast expanse of his comprehensive bosom. How I exult there—how I foam and sparkle. . . . I have as yet found no limit to this.

Nor had he. "Life now heaves and swells beneath me," is how he put it, "like a brim-full ocean."

Ebe was implacable. She never visited the Old Manse. Later, when Ebe occupied a house with the married Hawthornes for two years, Sophia said she saw her once. Ebe claimed that with the advent of his wife, her brother never wrote so well again. When he died she blamed her sister-in-law for keeping him too long in Rome. As an old woman she would still say that Sophia "is the only human being whom I really dislike." By then the widow was eight years gone. "That makes no difference."

But the shadows did not stretch from Salem to Concord. The newlyweds lived in idyllic seclusion, interrupted by distinguished company. Partly because of Sophia's enthusiasm for them there was, for her husband, rather too much of Margaret Fuller and Emerson. He disliked her and could not read him, who could not read Hawthorne. They took a walking trip together but were never close. Hawthorne preferred Thoreau, and the first time this prickly original dined at the Manse he sold the new occupant the boat he had plied for *A Week on the Concord and Merrimack Rivers* (1849). (It set Hawthorne back seven dollars, but Henry threw in a rowing lesson.) "Truly married," as she wrote, Sophia was discovering the capacities of that "wondrous instrument" the human body. She miscarried after a fall, and then in March of 1844 gave birth to a daughter named Una.

Released from Salem, from Castle Dismal and his room in it, the author did not discover in Paradise any compulsion to write. As Ebe might have predicted, only three significant tales issued from his three years' residence. "The Birthmark" is, from a radical slant, the work of a newlywed. "The Artist of the Beautiful" and "Rappaccini's Daughter" have protagonists who are richer developments of Oberon-Fanshawe; the "Daughter," Beatrice, represents the first seductive but frightening, exotic "Dark Lady" of Hawthorne's fiction. But the immediate problem was financial. He was not making enough to live on, was owed money for what he had already published, and had lost more on Brook Farm. The way out appeared to be a four-year appointment to surveyorship of the Salem

Custom House. On June 22, 1846, both a book and a boy were indeed delivered to the world— the second collection of tales, *Mosses from an Old Manse*, and the second child, Julian. Then the Hawthornes were dragged back to Salem.

But with a different house for the family, which now included Hawthorne's mother and both sisters. He served efficiently at his post until June of 1849, when a local political tempest sent his name "ringing through the land," Sophia said, and he was removed from office. The death of his mother the next month was to him more disturbing; it was one of but two times in his life when he is known to have broken down. "I love my mother," he wrote in his notebook, "but there has been, ever since my boyhood, a sort of coldness of intercourse between us, such as is apt to come between persons of strong feelings, if they are not managed rightly." Kneeling by her bed and holding her hand a long time, he "shook with sobs." It was surely, he added, "the darkest hour I have ever lived." He then came down with what Sophia called brain fever. It was she who nursed her mother-in-law, and she was busy decorating lamp shades, books, and screens to make money. Friends of her husband sent un- solicited funds, which he later repaid.

He was writing *The Scarlet Letter*, much the best of his romances. It suffices for the moment to remark that the book features the most effective

and memorable of his dark ladies—the abundantly dark-haired, black-eyed, rich-complected
Hester, exotic, bold, and beautiful. It also presents
her somewhat wizardly old husband Chillingworth, and her pallid, nervous lover, the Reverend Dimmesdale, to whom she is superior in
courage and sexuality. It may not be entirely
clear why this is, as the author claimed, "positively a hell-fired story." But it is much the
deepest and most powerful of his book-length
works, the one that will stand with the best of
his tales. For the subtlety, penetration, and
modernity of its psychological understanding,
further, it is astonishing. (With Chillingworth,
Hawthorne sketches the portrait of a psychiatrist,
and in accounting for Dimmesdale's malady he
lays down the basic principle of psychosomatic
medicine, generations before the terms existed.)
Anticipating Melville in the belief that there was
a secret in his life, the author's lawyer, George
Hillard (mentioned by name in "The Custom-
House"), wrote to put the question: "How
comes it that . . . you have such a taste for the
morbid anatomy of the human heart, and such a
knowledge of it, too? I should fancy from your
books that you were burdened with secret
sorrow; that you had some blue chamber in your
soul, into which you hardly dared to enter your-
self." The damage caused by sins kept secret is
one of the book's subjects, and it obviously

moved the author. For some unknown reason, he wrote the whole romance, as his widow would one day tell Thomas Wentworth Higginson, in a state of unaccustomed anxiety: "There was a knot in his forehead all the time," she said. When he completed the final scene in which the minister at last confesses his guilt and dies, he read it to Sophia. Or "tried to read it, rather," he wrote later on, "for my voice swelled and heaved, as if I were tossed up and down on an ocean."

After having explained persuasively why Hester could not leave the site of her troubles, Hawthorne now prepared to leave Salem. "I detest this town," he wrote Bridge, and rented a small red farmhouse in Lenox with a striking view of the Berkshires. Once again there would be literary neighbors. Oliver Wendell Holmes for one, but soon and in particular the younger Herman Melville. The story of this brief but charged friendship is almost legendary. The rhapsodic, anonymous review of the *Mosses*, invoking Shakespeare himself ("At last," wrote Sophia, "some one dares say" it). The mystery of its authorship. A visit from Melville, who greatly impressed both Hawthornes. Discovery that the review was his. Epic conversations between the two men, Melville dashing "his tumultuous waves of thought up against Mr. Hawthorne's great, genial, comprehending silences"—Sophia again. Then Melville's letters to Hawthorne, containing some of his greatest prose—particularly as regarded his whale," now deeply influenced by his friend, to whom in "my admiration for his genius" *Moby-Dick* is inscribed. Melville's "unspeakable security" in learning that Hawthorne had understood (it is not known just what he understood) this "wicked" book. But Melville could not sustain, as Hawthorne never achieved, the pitch of mighty exuberance that went into his masterpiece and this relationship. And for whatever reason, the older man, always reserved, became remote. The two met only twice after that last letter, leaving Melville to feel rejection and disappointment for some forty years.

The House of the Seven Gables, another testament to the weight of the past, was built at Lenox. It returns to the Hathorne ancestors of "The Custom-House." Colonel Pyncheon—stern Puritan armed with Bible and sword, and the original villain of the book—reinvokes Major William, American progenitor of Hawthornes. Having condemned the first Maule to death for witchcraft, he has brought down the curse—"God will give you blood to drink"—said to have been placed on John Hathorne, the "witch judge," and his descendants even unto the author. The story is chiefly about the workings of this

hereditary curse, its "professed moral" being that
the wrong-doing of one generation lives into the
successive ones: the "moral diseases which lead to
crime are handed down from one generation to
another."* The plot also returns to seventeenth-
century Hawthornes in connection with their
claim to a vast tract of land in Lincoln County,
eastern Maine, purchased from Robin Hood and
other sagamores. The Pyncheons do not find the
deed to the territory until it has become worth-
less; some nineteenth-century Hawthornes
blamed their failure to possess the same area on
the malediction incurred by their ancestral judge.
In contrasting spirit, the romance introduces
Hawthorne's Fair Lady, counterpart to the dark,
in the cheerful, pure, and domestic Phoebe
(Nathaniel's nickname for Sophia). It also de-
velops the figure of the controlling wizard, first
sketched in "Alice Doane's Appeal"; the executed male witch who cursed the original Pyncheon
has passed his black art to his grandson in the
form of the mesmerism the author feared for his
fiancée. By means of it, Matthew Maule sym-
bolically reduces the proud, exotic Alice Pyncheon to sexual slavery. But in flat contradiction

---

* It is not clear that the author knew the curse was actually
laid on Nicholas Noyes. According to Julian, he spoke of it
"half fancifully and half in earnest" as directed at Hathorne.
At the least, he seems to have appropriated it as expressing
some truth about his own ancestral legacy.

of its alleged thesis the book is brought to a sun-shiny close. It was very well received.

As Hawthorne somehow cooled on Melville, he now turned heatedly against Lenox and his remote, uncomfortable house. "I hate Berkshire with my whole soul," he declared. From in-laws he rented a place in West Newton, Massachusetts, and wrote *The Blithedale Romance* (1852). Having abandoned the tale as a form and the past as a preoccupation, he looked to his own experience at Brook Farm for material. A feeble book, badly put together and to no particular point, its true subject appears to be "the tender passion," which was rife at Blithedale in "various degrees of mildness or virulence." (And of various kinds as well. This was an unconventional society, the author remarks, which "seemed to authorize any individual, of either sex, to fall in love with any other, regardless of what would elsewhere be judged suitable." Hence, presumably, the unusual tenderness between the two males of the romance, and between the two females.) It is an untidy work generally, but it assembles what turns out to be the author's essential cast of characters. Zenobia is the dark lady, an "enchantress"—passionate, exotic, dark-haired, and "experienced." (She has "lived and loved!") The fair lady is Priscilla, specifically "fair . . . modest, delicate and virgin-like," timid and dependent. The corresponding males were introduced in *Fanshawe*, then developed in "The Artist of the Beautiful," where they appear as the solitary artist and a blacksmith, who marries the girl and fathers the child. Now the artist is the "minor poet" Coverdale, vaguely descended from Dimmesdale and Oberon. Inept narrator of the romance and Hawthorne persona, he might be called the Pale Lover. He is mainly a watcher: "I peeped," he says; "I would look on, as it seemed my part to do." Hollingsworth is similarly derived from the manly Walcott of *Fanshawe* and the blacksmith. "Massive and brawny" ("What a man he is!"), he is Hawthorne's Hale Lover, sought after here by both ladies. (He is an *ex*-blacksmith, and, domesticated after marrying Priscilla, he loses the purpose that had propelled him.) By now it has become clear that mesmerism is Hawthorne's nineteenth-century equivalent for seventeenth-century witchcraft. One Westervelt, with "the wizard mark upon him," subjects Priscilla to his malign magnetism, though Coverdale fondly believes she never actually surrendered. The poet claims *he* loved her, but only after she is safely Hollingsworth's.

In Concord the Alcott house was now for sale. Hawthorne bought it and nine acres for fifteen hundred dollars, renamed it the Wayside, and moved again. Sophia was pleased to run into both Emerson and Thoreau, out front, on her first afternoon there. Her husband also liked the place, but his life was about to take a turn. His sister Louisa, after jumping from a burning steamship, drowned in the Hudson River. Arriving in Salem too late for the funeral, he went to ask his sister Elizabeth, who was living with a family on the coast near Beverly, to return to Concord with him for a visit. She declined. He soon arranged that she should have two hundred dollars a year from him.

Meanwhile he had agreed to do a campaign biography for Franklin Pierce, nominated by the Democrats for President. Pierce was unpopular with the Hawthornes' intellectual acquaintances and in-laws, but a close friend. The biography was written and published, the friend was handily elected, and the author was offered the consulship at Liverpool. It was the best-paying post in the foreign service, second in prestige only to that of ambassador to Great Britain. He wanted the money and took the job.

In July of 1853 a period of seven years abroad began for him and his family, which now included the last child, Rose. The plan was to save money in England, then to live for a while in Italy. But Hawthorne worked hard and effectively at the office, particularly on problems that arose from grim conditions of life in the American Merchant Marine. He made loans out of his own pocket to vagabonds in distress. For

two years, without believing in the cause, he
did all he could to help his poor countrywoman
Delia Bacon, out to prove that Francis Bacon
and others had written Shakespeare. He was
"civil to at least 10,000 visitors," and "I never
wish to be civil to anybody again." Celebrated,
however, as a literary man, he even took to speaking at dinners. He actually came to enjoy it,
having learned the secret. ("I charge myself
pretty high with champagne and port before I
get upon my legs.") He was a great success at a
Lord Mayor's dinner in London, though he'd
begun to think it "altogether a ridiculous custom
to talk in one's cups." He met the Brownings as
well as other famous people, and had a last con-
versation with Melville, who announced he had
"pretty much made up his mind to be annihi-
lated." "He has a very high and noble nature,"
Hawthorne wrote, and is "better worth immortality than most of us." But he had been
unable to land him a political appointment.

It was something of a second successful career,
lasting five years, for Hawthorne, who had not
renounced the first one. He took a considerable
interest in *Our Old Home* (1863), as his book
of sketches of England and the English would
be called, and he wrote a lot in his notebooks.
Storing up for future use, he made a "sentimental
pilgrimage" to Uttoxeter to visit a spot he'd
written of and would again—the marketplace

where Samuel Johnson had stood bareheaded in the crowd, doing penance for having disobeyed his father a half century before. He spent a night at ancient Smithell's Hall, where a legendary Bloody Footstep was implanted in stone at the bottom of a stairway. He was attracted to the story of an American adventurer who was searching for a portrait that would prove he was heir to an English estate.

Having actually saved the money, the Hawthornes left England early in 1858. The ex-consul quickly decided that Rome was a "stinking, rotten, rascally city"—which, he was assured, he would end thinking delightful. ("We shall see.") He was in Italy a year and a half, enjoying best a "delicious" stay in Florence, mixing with artists and writers, including the Brownings. The worst of it was that Una contracted Roman fever and nearly died. Her father spent endless hours in Roman museums and galleries, then composed lengthy accounts of what he saw there and elsewhere in the city. The son of Puritans, he objected to the nudity of the sculpture. But he was much attracted to the Faun of Praxiteles, which is suitably fig-leafed, and to "Guido's portrait of Beatrice Cenci," still so called though there are good reasons for believing the painting is not Guido's nor the subject Beatrice. She was famed for having long ago conspired in the murder of her father after having been seduced or forced by him. It was the most popular portrait in Rome, and the author studied it until it became oppressive, so "perplexed and troubled" he was not to penetrate its secrets.

He was writing another romance, which became his own *Marble Faun* (1860). Though set in Rome it is yet in part another study of the effects of sin, concealed and revealed—of a crime in the past and its burden. The new problem is that large amounts of "guide book" material, taken from the notebooks, are not digested or fictionalized—or adjusted to the symbolic romance, itself confused and unresolved in plot and theme.

Like the *Blithedale*, it presents new forms of familiar characters. Here are the farthest reaches of Hawthorne's paired females. Miriam is the darkest of his ladies: abundantly dark-haired like Zenobia, Hester, and Rappaccini's daughter Beatrice, and like them "exotic"—vaguely Oriental in appearance but of Jewish blood and, perhaps, "one burning drop" of African. She is an "ambiguous beauty" of "moody passion," whom one sophisticated critic repeatedly calls "oversexed." There is a mysterious guilt about her, some crime in her family past. Because she is intensely associated with the Cenci portrait, many have guessed that she is the guilty daughter or sister or half sister of a man who persecutes her until at her bidding her lover kills him. Similarly Hilda is the

most extremely fair of Hawthorne's fair ladies—
a pretty, sunny New England girl become excessively pure and Puritan. Kenyon is the palest
of lovers, an authorial persona and the voice of
the notebooks, but so faint a figure he scarcely
registers. His counterpart Donatello is half faun,
but the ardent and unfrightened lover of Miriam
as well, quite hale enough to murder her tor-
mentor and then, in a bit of transparent symbolism, immediately to consummate their passion
in "agony" and "rapture." The diabolical pur-
suer of Miriam is a sort of veiled and failed
wizard.

Much of the book remains a Baedeker to
Rome, and in the end the author did express a
sort of love of the place. Then the family returned to Concord and the Wayside. Emerson
arranged a welcome-home party, strawberries
and cream. Hawthorne took up his literary
friendships with Longfellow, Holmes, Lowell,
and particularly Thoreau—even as he called him
the "most tedious, tiresome, and intolerable" fellow alive. About the approaching Civil War he
was just as candid. Not "bigoted to the Union,"
he rather wished New England might be a nation
unto itself. The South could depart and carry
off slavery—which did not much arouse him—
with it. He had an opportunity, on the other
hand, to meet with Lincoln, and wrote of the
President with warmth and great discernment.

Then he dedicated *Our Old Home* to Pierce, who had achieved a new peak in unpopularity.

But Sophia had noticed that even before leaving Italy he was losing his zest. By 1861 she was reporting "depressed energies and spirits." He had become "apathetic . . . hopeless . . . unstrung." Equally unstrung his compulsive, near-desperate efforts to write at last a romance based on the "bloody footstep" he had seen at Smithell's—and, less obsessively, on the American claimant to an old English estate. Failed, unfinished fiction, this was published posthumously in 1883 as a tale called "The Ancestral Footstep" and a romance, *Dr. Grimshawe's Secret* (Grimshawthorne's?). Both returned to the past and its burden of sin—the inheritance not so much of a great estate as a great guilt in the form of a terrible and potentially ruinous ancestral secret, in which the protagonist is still "entangled." It is probably contained in an old document which rests in a dark and "dangerous" chamber occupied by a pale and nervous young man. In "The Haunted Mind" of long before, guilt and chamber were nearly identifiable; this time it is the author who equates them. The room is like "a deep recess of my own consciousness, a deep cave of my nature." On its threshold, sin has planted its signature with a bloody foot.

Part of Hawthorne's inability to harvest this material is attributable to the state of his health.

It was no small difficulty, further, that despite his fixation on the ancestral footstep and the awful secret in the family that it points to he could not decide what the secret was, could not think of a sin dreadful enough for it to symbolize. Worst of all was his reluctance or inability to go into an abyss of his own psyche—the blue chamber Hillard detected years before, which now Hawthorne himself, using Hillard's own words, said he "hardly dared to enter."

He never in fact entered it, and in 1861 put aside his efforts and undertook the theme of immortality on earth. From these exertions, two more failures were issued posthumously— *Septimius Felton; or The Elixir of Life* (1872) and *The Dolliver Romance* (1876). The former resurrects familiar faces. Septimius, a pale protagonist, is the last incarnation of Oberon,* and Hagburn is his heartier foil. Septimius' sisterlike fiancée Rose is transformed in the course of composition to a real sister so that he is freed— except that he is badly estranged—for the dark Sybil. Overfamiliar objects turn up as well, the awful footstep and family papers recording some ancient sin. Failing again, Hawthorne for the last

---

* It is time to remark that Oberon, as King of the Fairies, relates to Old High German Alberich or "elf-ruler," but that its etymology conveys the pallor of the Hawthorne persona with unexpected vengeance. Oberon also relates to the Latin *albus*, whence *albino*—cognate with the Greek *alphos*, whence *alphosis*, or "dull white leprosy."

time tried similar materials in the *Dolliver*, and failed more completely. Once more his own project frightened him, and in the same way. "I linger at the threshold," he wrote his publisher, "and have a perception of very disagreeable phantasms to be encountered, if I enter." By 1864 he could not write at all. The manuscript lay on the coffin at the funeral.

He had been suffering more than depression. Once Sophia reported that his white, haggard face was "deeply scored with pain and fatigue." He would not hear of calling in a physician, but did go for a walk in Boston with Oliver Wendell Holmes. Thus a doctor learned of the depression, of a severe boring pain in the stomach, and noticed a "great wasting of flesh and strength." He did not really wish to examine his friend, or have to tell him what was wrong if he found out. In hope that the trip might be good for him, Hawthorne was on his way to travel in New Hampshire with Pierce. They set out, and in Plymouth on May nineteenth Hawthorne learned from his friend that Thackeray had died the previous winter in his sleep. He remarked what a boon it would be to go without a struggle, and that night he went—taking with him, if he had one, his secret. A relative reported later that Holmes had suspected "the shark's tooth was upon him." Present thinking is that the malign bite had at last reached the brain. Burial was at

Concord in Sleepy Hollow. Thoreau had preceded him there, but Holmes, Emerson, Longfellow, Lowell, Whittier, and Pierce, among others, were on hand with the family.

"Happy are those who die and can be at rest," Elizabeth Hawthorne wrote Una. She was not well enough to attend the funeral, but lived in radical seclusion for nearly two decades before dying of the measles. After editing and publishing her husband's notebooks, Sophia took the children, now fairly grown, to Dresden. Later she moved to London, where she died in 1871 and was buried, near Thackeray, in Kensal Green. Una, who had been subject to mental collapse, had a physical one at the death of her betrothed; in the spirit of her namesake she entered an Anglican convent, died there in 1877, and was buried beside her mother. Rose married George Lathrop, future editor and biographer of her father, converted to Roman Catholicism, separated from Lathrop, and became Mother Alphonsa (cf. *alphos*), revered Servant of Relief for Incurable Cancer, until she died in 1926. Julian fathered nine children, published over forty books, and lived until 1934. Twenty-one years previously, convicted of a stock swindle, he had appeared at an Atlanta federal prison— in regulation prison garb, according to the newspapers—with "the number 4435 prominent on the breast."

TWO

Fictitious Characters

'Tis hard to say whether for Sacrilege
Or Incest, or some more unhear'd of Crime
The Rhyming Fiend is sent into these men,
But they are all most visibly possest.

—*Horace's Art of Poetry*,
THE EARL OF ROSCOMMON, trans., 1684

"A BOOK is the author's secret life," as William Faulkner once remarked. Maybe this is why the oft-told tale of Hawthorne's history arrives at no great untold truth. Hawthorne implied that it wouldn't when he observed that if we were to search for the heart of a writer like himself we would not find it in any knowledge of his habits, casual associates, or abodes. Instead of displaying the author, he said, these things hide him. "You must look through the whole range of his fictitious characters good and evil, in order to detect any of his essential traits."

Very well. If you want the writer, look to the books. The father invites what the son Julian wished to forestall—the creation of a hypothetical author from his works. And the propriety of the procedure, as far as Hawthorne is concerned, is not in doubt. The question is whether or not he could produce a whole cast of characters, or types of characters, and still, as he put it in "The Custom-House," "keep the inmost Me behind the veil." And if he had a reason for doing so.

But it is not by his characters alone that we shall know the novelist. Rather from everything that makes up the fiction, narrative to imagery. Besides, with Hawthorne, there is the problem that the very modes of operation—allegory, symbolism, romance—are veils to inner meanings, as well as mediums through which the deepest of them emerge. There is also the relationship of the "moonshiny spirituality" of his surfaces, as Philip Rahv called it thirty years ago in his "Dark Lady of Salem," and the "repressed undermeanings." Three decades before that, in his *Studies in Classic American Literature*, D. H. Lawrence was writing specifically of Hawthorne when he announced that "you *must* look through the surface of American art, and see the inner diabolism of the secret meaning. Otherwise it is all mere childishness." So look *into* the books, if you want the writer, and search out the secret sense.

If Hawthorne's surfaces are not always childish, they are generally chaste—fit for the young in school, where they are studied. His language, for example, usually conformed to the Puritan/ Victorian conventions of a spectacularly circumspect age. Voluntarily he changed *wash* to *cleanse, female* to *woman, sectual* to *sectarian.*

When they occur, illicit matters such as Dimmesdale's indiscretion with Hester Prynne have taken
place so far offstage it is sometimes difficult to
credit them. And when, rarely, Hawthorne ven-
tured out of bounds, he hid his tracks with such
care that he has not in all instances been discovered. Subterranean deposits of sexuality in
his work have, of course, been much mined—
notably by Leslie Fiedler and Frederick Crews.
But how dense he is with this element goes generally unrecognized. Some of his best established
scholars continue simply insensible of it, and
even easily corrupted readers may overlook more
than they notice.

For example the complexities of Priscilla, fair
lady of *The Blithedale Romance*. She is, according to the formula, "modest, delicate, and
virgin-like." Yet there is some mysterious, un-
virginlike "past." Hollingsworth urges friends
not to "pry further into her secrets," which is
precisely what author prods reader into doing—
to the point where it has been argued that she
was a prostitute Hollingsworth brought from the
city to Blithedale for rest and rehabilitation. If
this is a bit more clinical than Hawthorne intended, it is hard to say what he did have in mind.
Or with the emblems, remotely reminiscent of
Hester's, which he assigns to both dark and fair
ladies. Zenobia's is simply the exotic flowers she

habitually wears. But Priscilla's is "the very pretty silk purses" she made when she lived in town, where Mr. Moodie used to flash them at drinkers in the saloons he frequented, or from corners where he lurked. This is curious enough, but what is remarkable about these purses is their femininity. As Coverdale says,

> Their peculiar excellence, beside the great delicacy and beauty of the manu-facture, lay in the almost impossibility that any uninitiated person should dis-cover the aperture; although to a prac-ticed touch, they would open as wide as charity or prodigality might wish. I won-dered if it were not a symbol of Priscilla's own mystery.

If it is not, and if the symbol is not what it seems, what is one to make of old Moodie on the day he comes to Blithedale, and inquires of Hollings-worth and Coverdale, "Has there been any call for Priscilla?"

> His tone gave a sure indication of the mysterious nod and wink with which he put the question. "You know, I think, sir, what I mean."

If the *Blithedale* has never been banned from the public schools, Hawthorne wrote a few things that could be. Incest is at the open heart of his earliest fiction, where it shamed Alice Doane, and it restlessly haunts the final work. The whole of *The Marble Faun* is informed or misinformed by the Roman figure of Beatrice Cenci (1577–1599), famed in the nineteenth century for her father's abuse and for complicity in his murder. Its only interesting character, however, is Miriam, a dark beauty whose secret and identity are mysteries one is supposed to track down on the basis of divergent leads that wind up somewhere in the catacombs. "A man might drown himself," we are pretentiously warned, in plunging after her secret. She herself "fears to go mad of it!" But, as with Hawthorne's last works generally, the reader is in search of a secret to which the author is not privy. We never learn why she is chased by a man to whom she is in "terrible thralldom," joined by a bond forged in "some unhallowed furnace as is only kindled by evil passions and fed by evil deeds." The sound of her "real name" makes Kenyon paler than ever; we are meant to recall a dreadful contemporary event to which a woman was partner. But identifying it throws no light on Miriam.

The most promising clue to her mystery rests in her close connection with "Guido's portrait of Beatrice Cenci," which obsessed Hawthorne. It was "the most profoundly wrought picture in the world."* Miriam sees Beatrice as guilty of something never to be forgiven, while her expression becomes very like the portrait's. Beatrice instigated the murder of her father, Miriam of the model who hounded her. One is led to suppose that their motives were the same. But though there is no problem in believing that Miriam and the model have been lovers, there are no grounds for thinking they are relatives. On the other hand, the situation is tidier than Hawthorne knew. Beatrice and her father were assuredly relatives, but it is no longer thought they were "lovers." That grievance, as Corrado Ricci showed in his *Beatrice Cenci* (1923), was almost certainly the unavailing invention of the girl's defense counsel when she was tried for her part in the murder. The legendary portrait is not by Guido Reni, is not of Beatrice Cenci, and the story that produced its impact is groundless. Similarly, the "romantic mysteries"—Hawthorne's words—at the heart of *The Marble Faun* are empty. But just as Beatrice is as closely associated with incest as any female in history, so Miriam's guilt seems vaguely incestuous even as the story fails to establish anything of the sort.

---

* He was not alone. "At last, at last!" wrote Sophia in *her* notebook on first viewing it "after so many years hoping and wishing." Her husband thought its force mysterious and its depth unfathomable.

Unexpected suggestions of aberrant sexuality show up even at Blithedale. Hollingsworth, the ex-blacksmith who marries Priscilla, has developed into a man of ideas about social reform. But as the abnormally observant Coverdale remarks, "There was something of the woman" in him. When he tries to win Coverdale's support for his philanthropic scheme—which the poet quite unaccountably refers to as full of "loathesomeness"—the rugged reformer says, "There is not the man in this world whom I can love as I could you." Coverdale, unpredictably, feels as if Hollingsworth had

> caught hold of my heart, and were pulling it towards him with an almost irresistible force. It is a mystery to me how I withstood it. . . . Had I but touched his extended hand, Hollingsworth's magnetism would perhaps have penetrated me.

But, now characteristically, "I stood aloof."*

Hawthorne had of course remarked that Blithedale permitted individuals to fall in love

---

* In his *Melville* (1975) Edwin Haviland Miller argues that Hollingsworth is Hawthorne's portrait of that powerful writer, and that the probable reason Hawthorne broke off their friendship was a hypothetical advance by Melville, which Hawthorne repulsed. There is no question but that Melville, as the title figure of his long poem *Clarel* (1876), was once in love with Vine, who clearly represents Hawthorne.

regardless of gender, and this the ladies of the book vaguely illustrate. For quite a while, Priscilla has eyes but for Zenobia. She lies at Zenobia's feet, kneels in delight at her beauty, gazes into her face. ("It was the strangest look I ever witnessed," says the superwitness Coverdale, "long a mystery to me and forever a memory.") Priscilla takes one "magical" caress from Zenobia as a pledge of all she sought—"whatever the unuttered boon might be." ("We men," Coverdale later explains, are "too gross to understand" this "mysterious attraction.") And so "Priscilla's love grew, and twined itself" around Zenobia.*

The author's sojourn at Brook Farm and the romance he made out of it have been pretty thoroughly examined. His far longer stay at the Old Manse in Concord—with Sophia during the early years of their marriage—has for some reason never been much looked at in relation to the fiction he wrote and published out of that place and period, 1842–1845. Indeed the only

---

* In view of the old idea that Zenobia is based on Margaret Fuller, well known to Brook Farm, it is relevant to recall that it was she who wrote, "It is so true that a woman may be in love with a woman, and a man with a man." She insisted, however, that such love was "purely intellectual and spiritual." Emerson thought otherwise, remarking that the female friendships in which Margaret was involved were "not unmingled with passion, and had passages . . . of ecstatic fusing." He noticed how girls were "eager to lay their beauty at her feet"—as Priscilla at Zenobia's.

substantial tales he produced in a new and changed environment have not been examined even in relation to each other. Thus something curious is missed.

There is no question but that as newlyweds the Hawthornes were profoundly happy, physically and emotionally. Sophia pronounced their life "a perfect Eden," and her husband invoked the same concept repeatedly. He even wrote a sketch called "The New Adam and Eve" (1843). What is strange is that every one of the major tales he wrote during this period qualifies as sexually problematic. The first two, called "The Birthmark" (1843) and "Rappaccini's Daughter" (1844), focus with misgivings on women. The second pair, "The Artist of the Beautiful" (1844) and "Egotism; or, The Bosom Serpent" (1843), are concerned with a masculine difficulty.

"The Birthmark" was composed about six months after the author's wedding, and—being the story of a scientist who tampers with and destroys his bride—it does have matrimonial relevance. Aylmer has married the beautiful Georgiana and is shocked, as he had never been while single, by a small crimson birthmark on her cheek. It is the "visible mark of earthly imperfection" on an otherwise perfect being. In the shape of a tiny hand, it expresses the "ineludable gripe in which mortality clutches the highest and purest of earthly mould, degrading them into kindred . . . even with the very brutes." He wants to remove it chemically. Georgiana is troubled, since it may be that "the stain goes as deep as life itself." But since—for no reason given—it makes her the object of Aylmer's "horror and disgust," she agrees to the experiment. At first her husband underestimates the strength with which the blemish had grasped her being. "Agents powerful enough to do aught except to change [her] entire physical system" having failed, he concocts a draft that works. Georgiana is perfect, but she is dying. Her only flaw was "the bond by which an angelic spirit kept itself in union with a mortal frame. . . . Thus ever does the gross fatality of earth exult in its triumph over the immortal essence."

A powerful tale—but of something on the surface with a "secret" meaning underneath. Georgiana's birthmark is of necessity a symbol, else her husband's postmarital horror and disgust remain unaccountable. Similarly incongruous the notion that it is degrading, and connects her with the animals, who do not appear to have birthmarks. What is hard to explain is that no one seems to have seen what Georgiana's is a symbol of—except for her when she suggests that the stain goes as deep as life itself. That it does, as a facial imperfection cannot. Its nature is plainly periodic. To eradicate it is indeed and precisely to change her entire physical system; in fact it constitutes a change of life. The symbol is what it says it is: birth's mark, its sign, and a baby's hand.

"Rappaccini's Daughter" concerns a pale young man who comes down with an acute case of sexual desire complicated by an equivalent sexual fear. Beatrice, first and youngest of the dark ladies, is a terrible temptation to Giovanni (nominally a south Italian, but transparently the familiar New England protagonist, now abroad).* It is a perplexing tale, but the erotic charge is foremost. Beatrice embodies the dread romantic figure of Poisoned Beauty. Her father, a scientist who has developed a magnificent garden full of lethal plants, has experimented with her as well. Now immune to the fatal flowers, she appears deadly in her own right, to be "touched only with a glove." Giovanni watches her arranging a blossom at her bosom; a drop from a petal falls on a lizard, which contorts and expires. "Beautiful shall I call her," he cries, "or inexpressibly terrible?" In this condition, he learns that her garden has "a private entrance," and that "many a young man . . . would give

---

* Hawthorne *sets* the tale in Italy, so luridly un-American it is, and whimsically attributes it to "Aubépine," French for his patronymic. This is the only thing he wrote that is mentioned in the late Mario Praz's encyclopedic study of erotic sensibility, *The Romantic Agony* (1933).

gold to be admitted among those flowers." Gold
he gives, and moves along "obscure passages"
until, "Forcing himself through the entanglement
of a shrub that wreathed its tendrils over the
hidden entrance," he finds himself in a garden of
"fierce, passionate, and even unnatural" plants.
Beatrice grasps him by the hand; next morning it
bears the purple imprint of her fingers. The
young people speak in "gushes of passion when
their spirits darted forth . . . like tongues of long-
hidden flame." But sick with mistrust and fear,
Giovanni's love "grew thin and faint"—in a
word, impotent. In the end Beatrice dies, leaving
him with a question that might be put to any of
Hawthorne's faint-hearted males: "Was there
not, from the first, more poison in your nature
than in mine?"* Doubt of woman is the destruction of man.

Nothing lusher than this ever bloomed at Concord. Before a gorgeous—if unnatural—shrub,
which Beatrice calls sister, she

> threw open her arms, as with a passionate
> ardor, and drew its branches into an inti-

---

* Ancient superstitions about the blighting effects females can
exert on flowers and fruit trees have shown remarkable survival
value. In 1920 Bela Schick, who developed the test for diph-
theria, sought to prove that women periodically exude "meno-
toxins" injurious to plant life. When Georgiana touches
Aylmer's magical flower only to see it turn coal black, and
when the bouquet Giovanni throws Beatrice appears to wither
in her grasp, it looks as if a long-lived tradition had reached
at least the edge of Hawthorne's consciousness.

mate embrace—so intimate that her features were hidden in its leafy bosom. . . .
"Give me this flower of thine, which I
separate with gentlest fingers."

As her poison is suspiciously venereal, the plant
is plainly female—like the garden itself, whose
entrance Giovanni forces to no avail.

Hawthorne's lovers, particularly creative ones,
have special cause for fearing ladies of special
attraction. The reason for this is hinted at in
"The Artist of the Beautiful," which presents a
complex struggle between the areas of artistic
production and of practical affairs. It has, however, a small and revealing sexual dimension.
Owen, a delicate craftsman, is pitted against
Robert, a brawny blacksmith who wins the girl
Annie and fathers the child. Robert "spends his
labor on reality." Owen, who is constructing a
mechanical butterfly that is virtually alive, in-
sists that his "force, whatever there may be of
it, is altogether spiritual." The clue to the un-
derside of the story lies in the special meaning
of two words, *spends* and *spiritual*, which may
be understood precisely as, for example, Shakespeare intended them when at the start of a
famous sonnet he defined "lust in action" as
"the expense of spirit in a waste of shame."
Robert expends his energy in smithing and
fathering. On the other hand, as Annie points
out, Owen is "putting spirit into machinery." To

achieve the beautiful, he must minimize expenses —save, not spend. This is Hawthorne's theory of "sublimation" roughly contemporary with that of his neighbor Thoreau, who wrote in *Walden* that the "generative energy, which when we are loose dissipates and makes us unclean, when we are continent invigorates and inspires us."

The complication is of course that the male who conserved energy during waking hours was liable to squander it nocturnally. The Artist is all too aware of this. It is for Annie's sake that he strives to "put the spirit of beauty into form." But her presence so excites him he cannot work —and then, he complains, "There will come vague and unsatisfied dreams which will leave me spiritless tomorrow." If that cannot be prevented, marriage can be. Owen has obviously faced Fanshawe's Choice, which had once been the author's: artistic creation or wife, book (butterfly) or boy. All chose the path of continence; Hawthorne waited until *Twice-Told Tales* was published before he married. Then, as if to thumb its nose at a bankrupt theory, *Mosses from an Old Manse* appeared on the same day as the boy, Julian.

"Egotism; or, The Bosom Serpent" exploits the spiritual element. It was written immediately after "The Birthmark," and both were published in the same month; never otherwise coupled, they make a striking pair. For "The Bosom Serpent" concentrates on what in Hawthorne's day, at least, was considered the curse of solitary manhood. Roderick Elliston has a live serpent in his bosom. A "lean man of unwholesome look" and "sickly white" complexion, he married, but has long been separated from his wife, Rosina. Estranged from all companionship, he is a gloomy fellow who steals abroad only in the dark. He is intensely morbid, and the cause of all this is "Egotism"—a monstrous self-absorption. About the terrible thing inside him he is profoundly ambivalent: its movements "gratify at once a physical appetite and a fiendish spite." Placed in an asylum for the insane, he only gets worse. "In solitude his melancholy grew more black. . . . He spent whole days . . . communing with the serpent." Affection for it mingles with loathing; "horrible love" and "horrible antipathy" embrace within him. Finally, in characteristic Hawthorne fashion, he is cured when he breaks off his sick self-contemplation by contemplating Rosina.

Suggested in this tale are many things, among them Invidia, or the deadly sin of Envy, Spenser's *Faerie Queene*, Edgar Allan Poe, and Jones Very, transcendental poet. But at its heart is the timeless symbol of the snake, and it is bemusing to see Rosina declaring at the end that "what it typified was as shadowy as itself." The type is glaring: solitary man in the grip of solitary vice. In the folklore of Hawthorne's day the figure was notorious: pasty-faced, friendless, depressed, mistrustful. Eventually he would go crazy. It was all spelled out in terrifying books and pamphlets. The Reverend John Todd's, cleverly called *Student Manual* (1835), went through twenty-four editions in twenty years. "Onanism," says the key chapter, not only robbed young men of physical and mental health, it deterred them from "the single-minded pursuit of the fixed path to success."* Marriage, if too expensive, would do the same. The whole economy has been called spermatic.

Thus it was not just artists and writers—Giovanni was neither—who worried about wasted substance, and so shrank from the dark lady. In varying degrees, all males caught up in a nineteenth-century Anglo-American spiritual structure shared it. To them had been newly

---

* Onanistic medical lore did not differ much from folklore. The British physician Henry Maudsley (1835–1918)—pioneer psychiatrist, author, and ex-Superintendent of the Manchester Royal Lunatic Asylum—composed a profile of the typical self-abuser (*Journal of Mental Science*, July 1868, 153–61) which reads like a second portrait of the Egotist in "The Bosom Serpent." According to Maudsley, the characteristic victim of the vice is, first of all, "egotistic." Like Roderick Elliston, he is "wrapped up in his own feelings." He is "morose . . . sullen . . . emaciated . . . solitary . . . shy . . . sallow . . . depressed, gloomy." He is also troubled with "anomalous sensations, and full of fancies . . . about his health." Hawthorne remarks that in blaming his troubles on a serpent in his bosom, Roderick might be

revealed a general truth about women—that (a) they feel only domestic passions, for home and children, and (b) they are sexually insatiable. This fractured knowledge informed and reinforced the older division of females into fair and dark, soothing nervous males with the one and worrying them with the other, impossible to appease.** Not of course that Hawthorne consciously endorsed such beliefs—or even the notion that females could be divided according to their coloring into the types that he, like other male and female writers, habitually delineated. But he and his fiction were sufficiently of an age that they fell into a pattern that he helped establish.

So does Roderick Elliston, the reduction to absurdity of his pale lover. Returning to "The Birthmark" with both him and Owen the Artist in mind is to throw an oblique last light, perhaps, on the obscure chemical researches of Aylmer, zealously scientific husband of Georgiana. The

"the victim . . . of a diseased fancy"; Maudsley's onanist has "positive delusions" about his physical condition, which he "attributes to mysterious agencies." Last, if Maudsley's afflicted male is sent to an asylum, as Hawthorne's was, he will, warns the former director of one, "invariably get worse . . . sink lower and lower in degradation," as Roderick did.

** An interesting treatment of such matters can be found in *The Horrors of the Half-known Life: Male Attitudes toward Women and Sexuality in Nineteenth-century America* by G. J. Barker-Benfield, 1976. The author believes (p. 272) that male sexual anxiety was so severe in nineteenth-century America that it contributed to a decline in the birthrate.

idea of an elixir of endless life appealed to Hawthorne for a long time. It is an ironic possibility that such was the nature of the potion Aylmer finally gave his wife: "a liquid colorless as water," it is specified, "but bright enough to be the draught of immortality." That could describe as well the spirit the Artist was anxious to store and the Egotist anxiously spent: the liquid, that is, through which man, in reproducing his kind, does achieve a form of immortality. It might occur to the reader that, rightly administered, it could have done away with the birthmark without destroying the patient. And that is about as far as Hawthorne's fiction can be taken.

"Every novel is some kind of higher autobiography," as Alberto Moravia told Saul Bellow. And the point has been demonstrated in unlikelier cases—such as Kafka's—than Hawthorne's. To read the latter with some knowledge of the life is to realize that there is not only a good deal of the erotic in his work, there is a good deal of Hawthorne. Transmuted and belittled, he is from the start to be found in his main characters. Fanshawe announced his plan for the future. Oberon and his ilk sketched a portrait of the artist as apprentice—in the pose he chose to assume for it. A pallid mask projected valid confessions: misgivings over the lonely path taken and the fiction no one would publish; dreams from a steeple of searching the hearts of men and women and penetrating their roofs to rooms where guilt is done; a nightmare of guilt staged in his own chamber.

More substantial tales are less subjective. "Young Goodman Brown," perhaps the most famous of them, tells of a young man's loss of faith in his bride, Faith, long before Nathaniel met Sophia, and might seem but distantly related to the teller. But Brown has scarce begun his disgraceful trip into the forest with the devil before we learn that he comes by this sort of thing naturally. He is the "very image" of the grandfather who made the same evil journey before him: the constable who "lashed the Quaker woman . . . through the streets of Salem," which is to say Major Hathorne as evoked in "The Custom-House," whose traits the author said he inherited. And it is here where the callow scribbler of "Sights from a Steeple," now standing in a congregation of the damned, is granted by the devil himself what he had longed for: power, in the devil's words, to "penetrate, in every bosom, the deep mystery of sin," to "scent out all the places . . . where crime has been committed"; he can "exult to behold the whole earth one stain of guilt, one mighty bloodspot." Here is a magical account of the origin of the author's insight into human culpability, and of his vision of the world.

His presence in the narrative core of "Alice

Doane's Appeal" is more obscure, and potentially more compromising, since at the heart of the tale is a forbidden sexuality. Leonard Doane's "diseased imagination and morbid feelings" have nothing to refer to but his love for his sister. He is quite aware that his "insane" jealousy of Walter Brome is born of the realization that Walter can love Alice with a passion denied him as a brother—for none of them knows yet that the young men are twins. Leonard and Alice have lived in fervent affection and "lonely sufficiency" to each other ever since they alone appeared to survive an Indian attack on their family. Maddened when Walter somehow proves that Alice's "powerful interest" in him has been consummated, Leonard kills him. In the lifeless features of his victim, Leonard sees a look of "scornful triumph"—over the spectacular unveiling, it may be, of his own guilty passion. Then, as if in a dream, the murderer has a vision of something previously confused and broken in his memory. In Brome's dead face he sees the face of his father, dead on a bloodstained hearth. He hears the childish wail of Alice, staring with him into their father's countenance. Having killed Brome, he suddenly shudders with a "deeper sense of some unutterable crime, perpetrated, as he imagined, in madness or a dream."

Thus in what may be his earliest tale did Hawthorne launch a career with a young hero who

has committed fratricide in fact, patricide in
fancy, and incest in his heart. Thus did he also
expose himself to the reader who would eventually relate Leonard's fragmented memory of his
father's death, and of Alice's girlish cries, to the
day when Nathaniel was four, and Elizabeth six,
that they were summoned to their mother's room
to learn that suddenly their own father was gone.
Intensifying the tale is the fact that Leonard and
Walter are even closer than twins—"like joint
possessors of an individual nature." Thus Leonard
has killed off not so much a brother as that side
of himself that fulfilled the desire for Alice. And,
having eliminated his only rival, while feeling
unaccountably involved in his father's murder,
he realizes that it was only through the sudden
death of his parents that Alice became his: hers
was "the love which had been gathered to me
from the many graves of our household!" For
Hawthorne, then, the fantasy is very close to
home—to the death of the seafaring father that
was accompanied by the virtual disappearance of
the reclusive mother, which isolated the son and
the sister who strikingly resembled the mother,
but at an age close to his own. Thus might they
live in lone sufficiency to each other, with a
younger sister who was very different, amid
relatives uncongenial. It is not strange that the
anonymous author should bury the tale in silence,
or that his outspoken sibling should remember

fifty years later that it possessed his peculiar genius.

If Leonard's fantasy of his father's death does somehow refract Hawthorne's "memory" of his own father's demise, this is the only place where he appears to have made even so indirect a reference to that parent. But in two very early and great tales there are hints of symbolic or substitute fathers. "My Kinsman, Major Molineux" tells of a country youth, Robin Molineux, who comes to town one night in search of a highly placed relative who may give him a start in the world. This kinsman is a figure of considerable status and power, but Robin has great difficulty in finding him. And when he finally does, it is in absolute humiliation—tarred and feathered and being ridden out of town by a savage, laughing mob. At first appalled, Robin is himself suddenly seized with "mental inebriety" and starts to laugh loudest of all. Shaken and subdued after the hideous procession passes, he will apparently take the advice of a gentleman who suggests that instead of returning home he remain in town a while, and perhaps rise in the world without the help of his kinsman.

Robin's is a mythic journey, beginning with a ferry crossing and climaxed with a ritualized sacrifice of a ruler or scapegoat by a rebellious populace that is acting out his own totally repressed wishes. Uncontrollable laughter betrays his astonished relief in discovering that the embodiment of authority—the people's and his anticipated own—is gone. He had made many "mistakes," in trying to find the Major, for the now-familiar reason that he did not really want to. This is a passage from youth to the threshold of maturity, accompanied by nightmarish anxieties and ending in the destruction of the father who stood in the way of his own adulthood. As a hereditary crime on which to base one of his last, unfinished romances, Hawthorne would one day consider "each son murders his father at a certain age." And though the story is probably set in Boston in 1765, with the Sons of Liberty overthrowing a Tory ruler in defiance of the Stamp Act, it is also based in the author's boyhood, where he too had a substitute father in the person of his uncle Robert Manning, at whose initials Robin Molineux's point. "My Uncle Molineux" was the story's title in manuscript, and it was born of a period when an independent-minded youth was subject to the decisions of his mother's brother. It is a bit of retrospective wish fulfillment.

Also based on a historical incident and redolent of myth, "Roger Malvin's Burial" can be tuned to a similar overtone. The title character is another older man, who himself bears Uncle Robert's initials. Mortally wounded in a remote wilderness, he finally persuades young Reuben (very like "Robin") to abandon him lest they both perish and leave Malvin's daughter—to whom the young man can be "something dearer than a father"—alone in the world. With mixed feelings Reuben departs. He marries Dorcas, and takes over Malvin's farm. That is but the start of a marvelous tale which ends in expiation of the guilt into which Reuben unintentionally fell, but already the familiar outline is visible. The young man is, in effect, rid of a figure who habitually called him "my boy . . . my son." (In Hebrew, Reuben means "behold, a son!") His response was, "You have been a father to me." With the father gone, the daughter, by extension a sister, becomes the wife. Three fathers have been supplanted in these early tales, and two daughters freed for brothers. Altered but audible are the vibrations of an ancient triangle.

Fathers removed, forefathers remained—and reappeared. Hawthorne took pride, along with the sense of inherited guilt, in the "dim and dusty grandeur" of his founding ancestors, but eventually he tired of their weight. Occasional spokesman for the author in a liberal mood, Holgrave in *The House of the Seven Gables* complains,

> "Shall we never, never, get rid of this Past . . . ? It lies upon the Present like a giant's dead body . . . just as if a young giant were compelled to waste all his

strength in carrying about the corpse of
an old giant, his grandfather, who died
a long while ago."

Of course it was the thesis of the book that the
past cannot be unloaded: "Bad passions . . . are
handed down from one generation to another"—
the author in his conservative mood. With
Colonel Pyncheon and his descendant the Judge,
this holds true. But what we observe about the
author himself, in his treatment of these characters, is the evident relish with which he com-
mits a species of ancestricide, killing them off.
For Colonel Pyncheon as described—"black-
cloaked . . . steeple-hatted . . . stern," and progenitor of his American breed—is indistinguishable from Major Hathorne as described in "The
Custom-House." Combined as one man with
the Colonel is the Major's son, the Hathorne
"witch judge" thought by some to have incurred the wizard's curse, of which the Colonel
dies. So, of "blood to drink," does Judge
Pyncheon, an event the author enjoys sufficiently
to spend a whole chapter on the corpse. (While
he is at it, he takes another swipe at his substitute
father, attributing Manning's great success with
pears to the Judge. As a private irony, he also
praises the "severity" with which the pomologist
"frowned on, and finally cast off, an expensive
and dissipated son.")

With even the unprepossessing minister of *The Scarlet Letter* Hawthorne formed a couple of personal ties. When in a chapter called "The Interior of a Heart" Dimmesdale passes night after night "viewing his own face in a looking-glass," in "constant introspection," he is doing exactly as the author did in a sketch called "Monsieur du Miroir" (1837), when he whimsically pictured himself as seen in a mirror, and studied the "impenetrable mystery" of his features. In the privacy of his quarters, indeed, Dimmesdale is suddenly indistinguishable from the tortured occupant of the dark chamber of "The Haunted Mind," who watches the mournful shades of his sins glide by his bed, until the finger of guilt pointed straight at his breast. In both scenes, the room's interior is the same as the heart's. Déjà vu—Dimmesdale watches a parade of spectral figures as they appear in his looking-glass. "Diabolical shades" sorrowfully "glided" through his ghastly chamber. The last is that of "Hester Prynne, leading along little Pearl . . . and pointing her forefinger . . . at the scarlet letter on her bosom, and then at the clergyman's own breast."

As close at this, at least once, the author felt to his invented clergyman. He must also have felt, at times, a relationship to his heroine Hester, for in reading Salem history, it is unlikely he would have missed its liveliest repository, the records of the Quarterly Courts of Essex County, stored in his hometown. There he could have seen a faded 1668 entry regarding a young woman named Hester Craford who confessed to fornication with John Wedg. "The judgment of her being whipped" was "respitted" until the birth of her child, when "it was left to the Worshipful Major Hathorne to see it executed."

Of more significance, if we understood it, would be the writer's relationship to Hester's *A*. The reader accepts it as essentially the sign of her sin, though Hawthorne never mentions the word *adultery*. Its "mystic" or "deeper" meaning may escape both author and audience of "The Custom-House." But when he places it on his own chest, and shudders and lets it drop like red-hot iron, it is much as if a finger of guilt had pointed once more at Hawthorne's breast. Much less mysteriously, it is through Hester that Hawthorne best expresses his personal sense of the force of Place, as well as Past, in both their lives. It may seem surprising, he admits, that his heroine—free to go where she would, without the stigma on her bosom—should remain where she was "the type of shame." But "there is a fatality," he explains,

> a feeling so irresistible and inevitable that it has the force of doom, which . . . compels human beings to linger around and

haunt, ghostlike, the spot where some great and marked event has given the color to their lifetime; and still the more irresistibly, the darker the tinge that saddens it. Her sin, her ignominy, were the roots which she had struck into the soil. . . . The chain that bound her here was . . . galling to her inmost soul, but could never be broken.

Here then she stayed, and here returned years later, still wearing the letter. So, Hawthorne had explained in his Introduction, with him and Salem, to which he had returned. Its hold on his affections was stronger than he'd known. "Though invariably happiest elsewhere, there is within me a feeling for old Salem," which is "probably assignable to the deep and aged roots which my family has struck into the soil." Understanding what he says about Hester makes it hard to wonder if no dark Salem event ever colored his life, and if he never unearthed anything sinful or ignominious pressing on his roots there.

In any case, his books declined steadily in value as he became more distantly related to their characters. In *The House of the Seven Gables* there is still a good deal of him. "The artist" Holgrave, who has "spent some months in a community of Fourierists," which reasonably describes Brook Farm, sometimes reflects him directly. And Phoebe Pyncheon, whom he is going to marry, is Nathaniel's portrait of Sophia, as well as the most fully developed of his fair ladies.* If not truly beautiful she is "very pretty," and graceful as a bird. As befits her type, she is profoundly domestic; indeed she transforms domesticity, gilding "even the scouring of pots and kettles . . . with an atmosphere of loveliness and joy." Further, the story Holgrave tells of her ancestress Alice Pyncheon suggests why during their courtship Hawthorne had such objections to Sophia's hope of curing her headaches by means of mesmerism. This new black art has been inherited by the grandson of the condemned wizard who originally cursed the Pyncheons, and by means of it he reduces the proud Alice, via the imagery, to sexual slavery. Bewitched, she is helpless in the hands of the hypnotist.

Hereditary evil and an oppressive sense of the past having worn out by the end of the *Seven Gables*, Hawthorne then wrote his sunnier *Blithedale Romance*, based on the recent experience of some months spent in a community of Fourierists. His art began to deteriorate more rapidly. It is hard to become any more engrossed

---

* The fair lady is seldom so striking as to be actually blonde, though her hair is never really dark and she is always light complected. Sophia and Phoebe had brown or brownish hair.

in his community than in the story he seems to have had vaguely in mind but never really told; what interest may be aroused lies chiefly in the standard characters, here assembled and altered. A minor poet, Coverdale is a near-bloodless on-looker. A furthest extension of the wishful young man in search of sights from a steeple, he has a secret perch in a tree at Blithedale and a post at a window in town, where he spies on both the book's females. He is a voyeur, the reduction to impotence of Hawthorne's observer. He counts a glimpse of Zenobia's shoulder, or part of her bust, a great piece of luck. He exults to think that "wedlock has thrown wide the gates of mystery" for her. "There is no folded petal," he exclaims pointedly, "no latent dew drop in this perfectly developed rose!" Contemplating Priscilla's "maidenly mystery," on the other hand, he "could not resist the impulse to take just one peep beneath her folded petals." But only in pursuit of his calling is he reckless.

In Kenyon, the sculptor in *The Marble Faun*, there is little life of any kind. He directly repre-sents Hawthorne, speaking right out of the Italian notebooks, paraphrasing sentiments or re-producing the sightseeing: it is as if in assuming his own character the author never thought to create one for his artist. Hilda, moralistic New England copyist, is another version of Sophia, but a fair lady who has fairly lost her appeal. Mrs. Hawthorne objected to the identification, but Hilda and Kenyon marry, and as unflattering refractions of their originals they more or less deserve each other. It seems much as though the author, in the gloom that was beginning to gather about him, was tiring of himself as romancer, and of his wife as well.

In any event, Kenyon, though Hawthorne's voice, may reveal less of his essential maker than do the feeble and somewhat faceless personas of his final, failed fictions. The first of the last romances were collected in 1977 as *The American Claimant Manuscripts*, a volume in which are printed, just as the writer left them, "The Ancestral Footstep" and two versions of *Dr. Grimshawe's Secret*, now called "Etherege" and "Grimshawe." The footstep is of course the bloody one, emblem of ancient family sin— which is "some mystery of a peculiarly dark and evil nature," perhaps contained in an ancestral document. Middleton, the pale protagonist, is tangled in it. But we never learn its nature, though it would seem to have nothing to do with the sins of founding Hathornes.

Interest in a nameless crime is impossible to sustain, but quickens a little when Hawthorne suddenly relates it, through Middleton, to a "blue chamber." This is of course the place his friend

George Hillard thought he detected in the author's soul, a region he feared to enter for the secret hidden there. In "The Ancestral Footstep" it is a bedroom, which Hawthorne soon refers to as "the Haunted Chamber"—another bedroom, which once appeared interchangeable with "The Haunted Mind." Familiar names, familiar rooms —across which, all unannounced, "Alice Doane's Appeal" casts a long and long-unnoticed shade. Middleton is involved in the killing of a man who lies dead with a look of joy on his face. Staring at his victim with a girl named Alice, he asks, "Whence this expression? Alice, methinks . . . we are members of one family." Then he adds cryptically, "How strange this whole relation between you and me." This threesome seems secretly what the Doanes and Brome turned out to be explicitly—siblings with one brother dead at the hand of the other. Later on a situation like this is mentioned as a criminal origin for the footstep.

Middleton and Alice reappear in "Etherege" as Ned and Elsie. Orphaned like the Doanes, they have been raised as brother and sister but with "a strange sweetness in their intercourse of which the fraternal relation is not susceptible." The plot is still groping for some old and awful family scandal. Brothers quarreling over the affections of a cousin won't do. Neither will a crime "which out of delicacy to the family the author was reluctant to state." ("I can't get hold of it," Hawthorne complains in an aside.) As an adult, Elsie is strangely moved by memories of the past. "This is wild," she tells Ned darkly. "It is best we should meet as strangers and so part." ("I don't advance a step," he protests this time.) Struggling in the dark, he once more approaches that

> chamber, which when I think of it, it seems to me like entering a deep recess of my nature; so much have I thought of it and its inmate, through a considerable period of my life.

It is "dim, dim" there—so dim the face of a "dearest beloved one, would be unrecognizable across it." Its occupant is pale, pale—"so pale that really his face is almost invisible in this gloomy twilight." Again a "devilish" influence is alive in the room; there is "a spell on the threshold." Thus "Etherege" backs off. And "Grimshawe" does not go beyond it save for the remark that to Ned, Elsie was "childhood, sister-hood, womanhood." Not since Melville's *Pierre* had anyone blurred the distinctions like that.

The Elixir of Life Manuscripts (also 1977) collects the late variations on the theme of im-mortality: "Septimius Felton," "Septimius Nor-

ton," and "The Dolliver Romance." Though a
little Indian blood makes him superficially dark
at times, Septimius is the faint lover of the golden-
haired Rose. The Redcoats have just marched
into Concord, and without apparent enmity or
volition Septimius has shot a British officer—
who, dying, calls him brother. In turn, Septimius
grieves for him as for a brother. This time the
face of the corpse registers joy and surprise. And
suddenly Septimius feels a "thrill of vengeful
joy," for the dead man, echoing Walter Brome,
had done what Septimius yearned to do: he had
kissed Rose. Finally Septimius does the same,
with unexpected results. In their embrace he felt
"something that repelled." As for Rose, the kiss
made her "shiver, even while she came the closer
for that very dread." But they are not supposed
to be siblings.

The British officer had given Septimius an old
document, which the American cannot make out.
Also figuring in the story is a dark lady called
Alice—then Sybil Dark, finally Sybil Dacy. She
tells the tale of the bloody footstep, which
Septimius relates to his first American ancestor—
who is, again, clearly no Hathorne in the author's
mind, being a man *hanged* for witchcraft, following a precipitate disappearance in this country. Then, as if the author were last to know, it
emerges that Rose and Septimius are indeed sister

and brother. Except perhaps for her unconscious wishes, that frees Rose to accept a hale and hearty suitor. And Septimius should be free to pursue the dark Sybil. "Why," asks Hawthorne, "could Septimius not love too?" And answers, "It was forbidden."

"Why?" asks the reader, incredulous that it should be for the reason that disqualified Rose. But that is how it looks. "We have an intimate relation to one another!" she tells him. At the "mutual touch of their two natures" he feels his soul "thrill, and at the same time shudder." A sudden shock and repulsion come between them. This continues until all at once its sense dissolves in the revelation that they are *not* kin; the new trouble is that the "brother" Septimius shot had been Sybil's lover. "I had given him all," she says, "and you slew him." Vaguely reminiscent of Leonard Doane, Septimius has killed the brother who possessed the sister Sybil never quite became—or failed to remain. She dies on the same spot as her slain paramour; *her* face wears a "malign and mirthful expression." It is as if all these death masks took wicked pleasure in knowing what secret sin the sexually bedeviled protagonist is drawn to.

The aged document passed to the unheroic hero, finally, was a formula for an elixir of life. But though "Septimius Felton" is nearer completion than the other last romances, it never gets round to doing much with the mechanics of immortality. The topic is to the *Elixir* manuscripts what the pursuit of an English estate was to the *American Claimant* drafts, a makeshift that does not support even a dwindled and bewitched cast of characters. "Septimius Norton" is but a protracted attempt on the same materials as "Felton." And at the end of the line "The Dolliver Romance" is of close to no interest at all except for showing—in some notes he made for it—that Hawthorne was at the last thinking of his heroine as "Alice," which was her name in the first place.

THREE

Fathers and Sons
and Lovers

*I am glad to think that God sees
through my heart; and if any angel
has power to penetrate into it, he
is welcome to know everything
that is there. Yes; and so may any
mortal, who is capable of full sympathy, and therefore worthy to
come into my depths. But he must
find his own way there.*

—Hawthorne to Sophia Peabody,
February 27, 1842

THE characters in a writer's fiction may
point, as Hawthorne suggested, to some of
his "essential traits"—if the characters are essentially or distinctively his. This is frequently
not the case. Literature must have started out, as
anciently urged, imitating life, but before long
it was imitating itself. Every type of fiction from
metrical romance to modernist novel has developed conventional figures, many of whose
traits owe more to tradition than to the character
and personality of the author who employs them.
Even Hamlet has been called a "stock character": a "high-thinking, vengeance-seeking
Hero" out of Elizabethan Revenge Tragedy. So,
for example, with Hawthorne's dark ladies. It
may be reasonable to consider, as many have

done, his ambivalence toward these several females for insight into his basic feelings about
women. But at the other end of the spectrum will
be found Perry Miller, who claims that all Hawthorne really had in mind in creating these characters was the heroine of *Corinne*, a once admired
novel by Mme de Staël. Hawthorne's dark lady,
says Miller, "owed all her being to his imagining
a Corinne in New England."

Since half of Hawthorne's dark ladies are
imagined not in New England but in Italy, which
is where Corinne is located, the point is not well
made. But it is aimed at a truth, a more ambitious
overstatement of which would be that Hawthorne's characters are essentially Scott's. His
male protagonists may display or distort some of
his own characteristics, but figures very like these
men can be found earlier in the romances of Sir
Walter. And there are more dark ladies in Scott
than in Hawthorne.

Scott was a special favorite, and early. Hawthorne read *Waverley* at fifteen, and it left its
mark on *Fanshawe*. Soon he had read all the
romances except (for reasons unknown) *The
Abbott*. While living in England he visited the
Scottish Highlands and "luxuriated in the scenes
long associated" with the books. By 1861 he had
all the Waverley novels; Julian remembered with
what relish he read aloud from them. His "pale

lover" is his particular version of Scott's so-
called passive hero (who is fair). His occasional
"hale lover" is Scott's "passionate hero" (who is
dark). Just as the pale lover, himself normally
passive, is not much of a lover, neither is the
passive hero especially heroic, though he loves.
And as Hawthorne had misgivings about his foremost character, so Scott—once, hypercritically
—called Edward Waverley "a sneaking piece of
imbecility." His passionate hero, on the other
hand, is strong, natural, and sometimes tragic.
Except for witches and wizards, all Hawthorne's
recurrent, standard characters fall easily into cate-
gories developed earlier in the Highlands.

It all began with *Waverley* (1814), where the
passive, fair, and unheroic Edward has the title
role. The dark, passionate, vaguely Byronic figure
is Fergus. Equally conspicuous and well defined
are the female counterparts. Rose is extravagantly
fair—hair of "paley gold," skin like snow, complexion that appears transparent. Flora is dark
like her brother Fergus; the exotic touch is that
she is Catholic, her mother French. Waverley's
wavering attraction to both women constitutes
the love story. But just as in Hawthorne the
dark lady and pale lover would always constitute
a mismatch, Flora warns Edward that union with
her would be "ill-assorted." Besides, dark ladies
in Scott are not cut out for marriage either.

Edward realizes that Rose will make the better wife, and Flora, having given him her diamonds for his bride, retires to a convent.

In *Ivanhoe* (1819), dark Rebecca in the end gives her jewels to Rowena of the mild blue eyes, and herself to charity. Rebecca, "beautiful daughter of Zion," has sable tresses and the lovely bosom Scott regularly provides. Rowena's can blush when her face does, and Scott makes clear the implications of her coloring by remarking that, as physiognomists would expect from her appearance, she is personally gentle and mild. Norman knights seize both ladies. Rowena's captor complains bitterly that she causes a frenzy in others while remaining free of passion herself. Rebecca's Templar demands that she convert and submit, but knows she will leap to her death if he advances. Condemned as a witch and eventually freed, the most beloved heroine of the age suppresses her love for Ivanhoe, who marries Rowena. This so disappointed readers that thirty years later, in his *Rebecca and Rowena*, Thackeray remedied it.

But Scott stayed with the rules he helped establish. In *The Pirate* (1821) the dark Minna's element is night; attuned to nature, she is deep-feeling and noble-spirited. Her cheerful sister Brenda, who stands for "housewifely simplicity," can blush like Rowena. Fair lady marries dark hero; Minna is separated from her pirate lover when he is captured, and she retires to perform good works like Rebecca. There is a little twist to *Peveril of the Peak* (1823). Alice is like a sister to Peveril, whom she will marry, but she has dark hair. This is taken care of by the introduction of a darker beauty—Fenella, whose mother was a Moor. Both ladies are in serious sexual danger. Fenella, "born to gaze on the sun which the pale daughters of Europe shrink from," is unafraid. Both ladies love Peveril, Alice wins him, and only if Fenella is forgotten can everything be thought to turn out fine.

Perhaps readers forgot her, since it was all according to convention. But some had found unacceptable in *Rob Roy* (1817) a sharper twist. Rob Roy is the passionate hero, and Frank the passive one. He doesn't amount to much— especially as compared with the bold, beautiful, and accomplished Diana Verdon, who is dark, Catholic, romantic, and mysterious. She cannot join with Rob Roy, who is married and an outlaw to boot. There is no domestic lady, and so she marries Frank—to the dismay of Scott's critics: these lovers were "ill-assorted." Perhaps the critics were inattentive: on the last page of his book Scott parted the pair as he was supposed to. Diana, it transpires, died very quickly, apparently without issue. He followed the rules after the game was over.

Of course he had not invented it. Rousseau's

scandalous and influential *La Nouvelle Héloïse* (1761) came much before him. Hawthorne read it, in translation, "when I was hardly more than a boy" (because, according to his sister Elizabeth, "he was told he shouldn't"). The experience obviously sank in; as late as 1859 he noted in his journal how the book retained its hold on his imagination. And so very early he saw how, as Rousseau said, he imagined two women friends, and made one dark, the other fair. Julie is "*blonde . . . tendre, modeste*"; Claire, her cousin, is "*une brune piquante . . . un peu ornée.*" Their own erotic relationship enhances them in the eyes of the men.

A "true spiritual daughter of Rousseau" is what Perry Miller called Corinne. She was also a close female equivalent of the Byronic hero—and was, further, a model for Margaret Fuller, whom Emerson called "the new Corinne." The idea that Hawthorne created his dark lady by transplanting Corinne to New England does fit Zenobia of the *Blithedale,* who resembles de Staël's heroine as his other dark ladies do not.*

---

* An odd parallel between Ms. Fuller, later Mme Ossoli, and Mme de Staël involves the matter of femininity, which despite her legions of lovers the French writer was said to lack. So Margaret Fuller, according to Hawthorne, "had not the charm of womanhood." The great Talleyrand, burlesqued as a lady in de Staël's *Delphine,* observed, "It seems that Mme. de Staël has written a novel in which both she and I are travestied as women."

But it is not certain that even Zenobia is based on her. Following its translation in 1807, *Corinne* was, as Miller says, "assiduously read by middle-class daughters" (and "denounced from middle-class pulpits") across America. Thrilled by its glorious heroine, females of the age yearned for the glamours of Rome—the Coliseum by moonlight, and so forth. Sophia read the book when she was fifteen, and dreamed of the Eternal City long before Nathaniel did—if he ever did. It is hard to think he was much taken with the novel, which is slightly hysterical and stridently feminist. A couple of knowing references show, however, that he had read it by the time he wrote *The Marble Faun*. Both romances are fictions unsuccessfully wed to Italian travelogues. And *Corinne* is said to have influenced Scott, who influenced Hawthorne.

It assuredly influenced women; by 1872 the book had gone through forty editions. Its black-haired, dark-eyed tragedienne is a more complete dark lady than most of Scott's in that, like Zenobia, she is an "awakened" beauty who manages to seem both pure and possessed of a significant past. Lord Nelvil, her companion in Rome, is a classic pale/passive lover, in all ways her inferior. But attracted to him as well is her half-sister, the truly innocent, deeply domestic Lucile. Like Zenobia, Corinne is rejected and dies, leaving the male to the suitable fair one. Yet Corinne's remarkable distinction is that she is able to triumph from the grave. She had cursed Lucile's marriage by warning that Nelvil would never taste in her arms "one rapture that reminds him not of Corinne," then dies to put a seal on it. And so great is the power of her posthumous sexuality that when Lucile bears her husband a daughter, the child is not fair like her mother but dark like Corinne, and exists as a blight on the marriage.

Hawthorne was a man of great moral sensibility, and if he got to the end of *Corinne* he must have come to dislike its heroine quite a bit. His Zenobia may resemble her, but he was not much indebted to Mme de Staël. For that matter, whatever the similarities in design, his end product is not much like Scott's. The truth of the matter is that he differs a good deal from any of the sources that have been discovered for him, and no study of his fictional characters, let alone their origins, has ever penetrated to a significant revelation of his own personal essence. But there is another way of getting closer to that. It has been approached, yet not pursued to its somewhat unusual conclusion.

In life as in literature, Hawthorne was unique. Aloof, defensive, reserved even with intimates, he could on exceedingly rare occasion be spiritually generous, open, disarmed. Never at any one time were these contradictory and most unequal sides to his nature more deeply felt and clearly articulated than in the letter he wrote his patient fiancée in February of 1842, expressing his willingness for any fully sympathetic person to know everything that was hidden in his heart. But, he warned flatly, such a person—and surely Sophia, above all others, was such—could get no help at all from him.

How iron was the inhibition that prevented Hawthorne from expressing his deepest and most private feelings is never more apparent than in this letter and its resolution. It was here that he at long last agreed to tell his mother and sisters that he was going to marry. But Sophia had no idea, he wrote her, how difficult this was going to be. Directly he acknowledges the "abyss of my nature" and the "cloudy veil" he stretched over it. And completely he denies "any love of secrecy and darkness." It is rather that in his family

> there seems to be a tacit law, that our deepest heart-concernments are not to be spoken of. I cannot gush out in their presence—I cannot take my heart in my hand, and show it to them. . . . And they are in the same state as myself.

Characteristic of New England, it may strike some—if for unclear reasons. But for Hawthorne the family "incapacity of free communication" was "meant by Providence as a retribution for something wrong" in early dealings among its members. Whatever the cause, three full months passed and he had still not brought himself to announce his marital plans at home. Sophia finally did it in a letter. Ebe responded to the long silence with formal, icy rage.

As Sophia was the first to admit, she never did see into the depths that she knew her husband closed off. And so for those who would like to learn what was there it is fortunate that there was another mortal—enormously sympathetic to the reticent writer, and blessed in Hawthorne's judgment with "a high and noble nature"—who thought he did see into the abyss. When first Mrs. Hawthorne got to know him, Herman Melville impressed her every bit as much as he did her husband. "I am not sure," she wrote her mother, "that he is not a very great man." What struck her most was his "very keen perceptive power":

> Once in a while his animation gives place to a singularly quiet expression . . . an indrawn, dim look, but which at the same time makes you feel that he is at that instant taking deepest note of what is before him. It is a strange, lazy glance, but

with a power in it quite unique. He does
not seem to penetrate through you, but
to take you into himself. I saw him look
so at Una yesterday.

It is hard to think he never took Una's father
into himself. But it was more than thirty years
later that he told her brother Julian, who reported it in print for the first time in 1901, he
was "convinced Hawthorne had all his life concealed some great secret, which would, were it
known, explain all the mysteries in his career."
In saying this, Julian reports, Melville was ter-
ribly nervous. Perhaps he was not saying, nor did
Julian suspect, that he had long believed he knew
the nature of the secret. In fact he had already
published a transparent clue to it—without, so
far as is known, having attracted any attention
whatever.

The literary history, at least, of what Melville
thought he had discovered about Hawthorne is
simple. In his *Mardi* (1849) he had created and
juxtaposed his own dark and fair ladies along
conventional though semimythic lines. Three
years later, shortly after getting to know the
Hawthornes, he wrote his deeply troubled
Pierre, in which he drove the conventions at-
taching to these figures to the end of the road.
He sent a copy to Hawthorne, whose response—
unknown—was probably shock. It is a shocking

book. Pierre, apparently in love with his mother but engaged to the lovely blonde Lucy, yearns most for the sister he thinks he lacks. Because

> the wife comes later. He who is sisterless
> is a bachelor before his time. For much
> that goes to make up the deliciousness of
> a wife, already lies in the sister.

Soon he discovers that he has one, a half sister, in the darkly beautiful Isabel. Then Melville turns the whole tradition on its head. Pierre rejects his fair fiancée, literally embracing his sibling, and destroys them all. Further, as an unneeded signpost, Melville introduces into his romance, years before Hawthorne, a portrait of Beatrice Cenci. One year before Hawthorne, he had gone to the Barberini Palace to seek out the original of that painting. He bought an engraving of it, which is preserved, noting that "not caught in any copy" was the "expression of suffering about the mouth."

When almost twenty years later he published *Clarel: A Poem and Pilgrimage to the Holy Land* (1876), Melville had Beatrice and Hawthorne together in his mind. In this long and mostly unread work, the young Clarel represents Melville. He is enamored of a middle-aged American artist named Vine, who is clearly Hawthorne: a reclusive, reserved, nonparticipating observer,

moralist, and symbolist caught up in the past.
Vine rejects a "feminine . . . passionate mood"
in Clarel, and while Vine is off guard Clarel has
a dramatic insight into the expression on his face
—such, perhaps, as Mrs. Hawthorne witnessed
in watching Melville. Of Vine, the poet writes

> He wore that nameless look
> About the mouth—so hard to brook—
> That in the Cenci portrait shows,
> Lost in each copy, oil or print;
> Lost, or else slurred, as 'twere a hint
> Which if received, few might sustain:
> A trembling over of small throes
> In weak swoll'n lips, which to restrain
> Desire is none, nor any rein.

Clarel, according to an English reviewer of the
time, is a poem of "about twenty-seven thousand
lines, of which we can only say that we do not
understand a single word." There is, to be sure,
some awkwardness of expression. But what Melville is saying here is that around his mouth Vine
had a look, hard either to describe or accept,
that appears in the portrait of Beatrice Cenci,
though not (as noted in the journal) in copies of
it—or else is blurred, as suggesting something
few might bear up under if they perceived it:
little spasms in indulgent lips that have no
strength to hold back desire. There was no need

to say more. It was a tell-tale look. The crime symbolized by the Cenci portrait, as Melville's century saw and understood it, was needless to name. Thus Melville had expressed as clearly as he ever chose to—or should have needed to— what he took to be the nature of Hawthorne's "great secret."*

Beatrice Cenci, in both Hawthorne and Melville, relates to the figure of the dark lady. And it is generally assumed, thoughtlessly, that the origins of this mysterious female lie in the traditions, chiefly literary, both writers subscribed and contributed to. "Though the celebrated Dark Lady . . . haunts Hawthorne's fiction," a contemporary scholar observes, "she does not appear in his personal legend." That she does not, as it is presently shaped. But what is missing from a modern understanding of this writer is awareness of great gaps in that legend. And of the extent to which his fiction grew out of personal experience, vicarious and direct, which filled those gaps.

---

* It is likely that Melville had his deep perception of Hawthorne during their exhilarating relationship in western Massachusetts. His enthusiasm for his older friend was at the time boundless and reckless; his letters to him are electric with it. In the summer of 1851 he was finishing *Moby-Dick* in the same inspired mood; he was about to write *Pierre*, boldest of incest novels. It is conceivable that he mentioned its theme to the man whose "heart beat in my ribs and mine in yours, and both in God's"— as one that might interest them both. If so, this could have been what destroyed the relationship as it had been: the "shock of recognition," a phrase Melville had used in reference to his rapport with Hawthorne, that blew the circuit.

In somewhat the same way, the notion of an old, hidden family document, which contains a terrible secret involving an awful crime—still alive in the central character's own day, which the author in his last years could not leave alone —seems a piece of musty Gothic machinery left over from a previous age. An apparently tired fancy, it is little more likely to be credited—"believed in"—than the business of an elixir of life immortal which the same writer tried to profit from. So, less conspicuous, the concept of a sibling triangle, which his earliest tale is based on and his final fictions echo, seems an unaccountable invention for a son of the Puritans. But the truth is that neither the triangle nor the hidden document was an actual invention or a matter of literary borrowing.

Truth can be stronger than fiction. And though Melville may not have known it, there really was a Dark Lady of Salem. No part of Hawthorne's legend, she was deep in his life. "You must never expect to see her in the daytime," he cautioned. "I never imagine her in sunshine. . . . I really doubt whether her faculties . . . begin to be exercised till dusk. . . . Their noon is at midnight." He was writing his fair fiancée. Until he married her in middle age—his character formed, career far launched—the shadowy lady was closer to him than anyone.

She loomed large in that isolated household of unmarried Hawthornes on Herbert Street—all through the twelve postgraduate years in the room under the eaves where he said he was shaped, and in turn shaped visions he put before the world. She had been the kindred playmate of his childhood, "my sister E." Eighteen years had passed since she had, as if miraculously, appeared to him a child no more—"a tall handsome young woman," rather, so generally altered he did not know her. When he did, according to his sister L., also present, "he stood transfixed with astonishment."

The exact coloring of Louisa, the younger sister, does not seem to be recorded. But in character and personality she was wholly fair—daytime to Elizabeth's night, domestic as her sister notoriously was not. Cheerful and compliant, she was fond of clothes and dancing. She was "fragile, pale, amiable," according to Julian, and "not very effective." Of Elizabeth, there has been found no likeness, but with long black hair and gray eyes she is said to have inherited her mother's dark beauty. Older, more precocious, individualistic, and forceful than Nathaniel, she paved the paths into which he was drawn: solitary meals and walks, nocturnal reading and writing. Never venturing beyond her tiny sphere, she harbored few illusions as to what was out there. It was "only through books," her brother remarked, but "she knows the world marvelously."

Her own literary career, such as it was, aborted. Only thirteen when she left school, she nevertheless translated the whole of *Bon Jardinier* for her pomologist uncle, and several of Cervantes' tales. What she actually published was unsigned and unrecognized. When he edited *The American Magazine* she was Nathaniel's only contributor. A Whig who argued politics with her brother, she wrote a eulogy of Alexander Hamilton. *Peter Parley's Universal History* molded American minds for more than half a century, promoting Christian theology and national chauvinism. It made a fortune for its publishers; "It is probable that the writing was entirely hers," according to one who has studied the matter. "Destitute of the ability to earn," as she observed, she was never engaged to review books as she would have liked. But two pages of *American Women Writers* are devoted to her, and an edition of her letters is in preparation.

"For everyday purposes of pot-hooks . . . and flat-irons," Sophia would write her mother, "Elizabeth is not available." If it was up to her to clean a room, it was not cleaned. If there was money, it went for books. Her brother, who so feared her disapproval as a young man, ended calling her "the most sensible woman I ever knew in my life, much superior to me in general talent." Tribute would come as well from both his daughters. "I never remember you to have told me anything twice," Una once wrote her aunt, "and that can be said of very few people; but there are few enough people in the least like you." Yet it was the younger Rose who left the most memorable recollection of "my recluse aunt." By 1897, when she completed her *Memoirs of Hawthorne* in which it appears, Rose had converted to Roman Catholicism, formally taken leave of her alcoholic husband, and was devoting her life to the physical care of terminal patients in cancer wards. She had lived a good deal abroad and had a perspective on the aunt who had lived so long at home alone. The first time Rose saw her, as she recalled it, Ebe was most uncharacteristically knitting. She did not at the moment seem "mysterious" or "romantic." Rose perceived instead the resemblance to her father: it was "magic." She had "the same eloquence in her silences; and when she spoke, it was with a sympathy that played on one's whole perception." Her power was unmistakable, and though she lived in "the utmost monastic retirement" she was "chock-full of worldly wisdom." She was also, wrote Rose, soon to be Mother Alphonsa, "a good deal unspiritual in everything," and "potentially rather perverse." But she possessed "loving-kindness of a lazy, artistic sort. . . . She was unregenerate, but excellent."

At least as much as Ebe loved books, she loved the woods. Rose remembered her best in them. There she was "quick and ardent," the

> great eyes peering and disappearing again. . . . Her dark brown, long lashes and broadly sweeping eyebrows were distinct against the pallor of her skin, which was so delicately clear, yet vigorous, that I felt its gleam as one feels the moon.

It was the eyes Rose remembered most powerfully, and not at all as most would recall the eyes of a maiden aunt. "There was nothing which her large, lustrous eyes could not see," said Rose, "and nothing they could not conceal." Ebe was as hostile to the idea of a biography of her brother as he was.

A footnote to the story of Elizabeth Hawthorne is that in her late sixties she took a strong stand on the lurid old rumor of Byron's incest with his half sister Augusta. In two sensational publications, which appeared forty-five years after the poet's death, Harriet Beecher Stowe had zealously undertaken to support Lady Byron in her charge against the reputed lovers. Studying the case with "a lawyer's precision," as some-

one put it, Ebe vigorously disputed the allegation.
Archly dismissing the poet's widow, she remarked that though persons of little imagination
ought to be free of idle fancies they are full of
them—and always those of an "annoying
nature."

Why she found the notion of incest aggravat-
ing, rather than disgraceful, repellent, or whatever, is not clear. Perhaps she thought it took
genuine imagination, or more knowledge of the
world than Lady Byron possessed, to invent such
a sin. The intensity of her interest in the whole
affair is unexplained, though as something of a
dark lady herself and an admirer of "Alice
Doane" it does not come, perhaps, as a total
surprise. That "the taint of incest" ultimately
attaches to the figure of the dark lady in literature
has been observed before now. On her first appearance in American fiction—as both dark
bride and "Mamma!" to the young hero of
Charles Brockden Brown's *Arthur Mervyn*
(1800)—the taint is very perceptible. With the
dark bride and half sister of *Pierre* it is the heart
of the matter.

In Hawthorne, to be sure, the stain is not generally visible. After Alice Doane, only Miriam of
The Marble Faun is cloaked in what Nabokov
called incest's "subtle perfume," and it evapor-
ates. It has never been argued that Beatrice

Rappaccini is related to Giovanni, or Hester
Prynne to Dimmesdale, or Zenobia to any man
at Blithedale. Timid lovers rejected these women
out of sexual fear, perhaps. But if there was anything forbidden in their embracing it could only
be attributed to the barely perceptible tendency
of Hawthorne's young men to see sisters in
females everywhere.

This was notably the case in the very beginning, but it is plot, not the symbology of dark
and fair, that revealed it. Alice Doane is not
physically described at all; it is essential to the
story, though it's later contradicted, that she has
been seduced by her brother Walter. Though
they were potential or imminent lovers in "The
Ancestral Footstep," another Alice seems very
like a sister to Middleton. Similarly Elsie to Ned
in "Etherege" and "Grimshawe." It is only in
the most substantial of Hawthorne's posthumous
publications, "Septimius Felton," that the dark
development in the action matches the symbolic
coloring of the heroine. When Alice, later Sybil,
of the "large, dark, melancholy eyes" tells Septimius they are closely related, and each shudders
to thrill at the touch of the other, nothing could
be more plain. The fact that the author again
contradicts what he has revealed does nothing
to obscure it.

And the final step is inevitable: literature imitates life, literature imitates literature, life imitates literature. Byron's incest has been called a plagiarism. The immediate applicability of this development is that whatever Hawthorne's characters may have owed Scott, his dark ladies do not resemble Sir Walter's more closely than they do his sister Elizabeth. Like Flora in *Waverley*, she strikingly took after the brother to whom she was long so near. Like Minna in *The Pirate*, night was her time, darkness her element, the out-of-doors her passion. Her eyes could look on what others shrank from, like Fenella's in *Peveril*. Ebe never left the tiny region of her birth but has been called an "exotic"; as her niece Rose implied, there was something romantic and mysterious about her. Not simply un- but anti-domestic, she was not, despite her attractiveness, cut out to be a wife. In line with the fate of dark ladies in literature, she was rejected for a fair one—at which point, following the formula, she effectively departed the world. "A good deal unspiritual," she could never have taken refuge in a nunnery, but a convent would have provided no more radical retirement than she chose for herself. If Scott's dark heroines were anomalous in being "inexperienced," that is not at all, as everyone observed, the way she seemed. Her sister appeared "innocent," she did not.

As Elsie represented to Ned "childhood, sister-hood, womanhood," so for many years Ebe to Nathaniel. So many things suggest a brother-sister relationship closer than normal, there is reluctance in drawing inferences which seem, paradoxically, too obvious to be valid. Phaedrus announced two thousand years ago that things are not always what they seem. But if they are not, what then is to be made of a sister's open and long-lived admiration for "Alice Doane's Appeal," with its vibrant biographical overtones? (That if they were relevant to her and her brother she would never have mentioned the tale? She was bold: how bold?) How much might be made of her instant, blunt, undying dislike of her brother's wife? Why the vigorous immersion in the details of Byron's relations with his sister, and the ex cathedra rejection of the charges? Closer to home, to what degree can a sister be made out in the shade of that pale beauty who came in sin and desolation to a young man in the bed of his haunted mind, or stood beside it guilt-stained as a demon pointed to his breast? If there is nothing of a sister there, is she among the female shadows of "Fancy's Show Box"—a type of sin never perpetrated, only the object of thoughts that pollute the heart? Have these apparitions in a haunted chamber nothing to do with Hawthorne calling his own place under the eaves "squalid"—which still may be defined as "morally repulsive"? In light of a sister's resemblance to a mother, might something more be made of a son's encephalitic reaction (Sophia's diagnosis) to the mother's death? Was the mysteriously injured foot, which as a boy crippled Nathaniel for two years, a Delphic sign that a better name for him than Oberon ("white leprosy") might be Oedipus ("swell-foot")? Fancy's Show Box runs amuck.

But facts, as Winston Churchill once remarked, can baffle the imagination. And they are not all in yet. An extraordinarily large one can be approached, once more, by way of *The Scarlet Letter*.

The court's charge against Hester Prynne in life, as Hawthorne probably knew, would not have been *adultery*, a word he never used either, in her connection, but "a lying together in the same bed," or something of that sort. Nor was punishment for it always the wearing of a symbol. The woman of Boston who came before William Hathorne in 1673 was given a choice. She could leave the colony, as Hester could have, or be whipped, then stand on a stool in the marketplace with a paper on her breast explaining that she was there for her ADULTEROUS AND WHORISH CARRIAGE. But the penalty could be more severe, as at the start of the book the townswomen wished it had been for Hester. In 1644 Mary Latham of Boston, married like Hester to an old man she did not love, lay in bed with "divers young men" and, according to John Winthrop, was executed. Sarah Pore of Salem, who like Hester refused to name the father of her offspring, was whipped, then jailed to be whipped once a month until she confessed him (after a month and a week). A few cases involved the birth of mulatto children to white women; perhaps Hawthorne knew that Martha Cory, that "unhanged witch" of "Young Goodman Brown," was one of them. It is a matter of record that he borrowed Joseph B. Felt's *Annals of Salem*, 1827 (second edition, two volumes, 1849), from the Salem Athenaeum in 1833, and again for three months in 1849 when he was writing *The Scarlet Letter*. Here, it is supposed, he found his symbolic initial, where Felt records that in 1694 a law was passed that those found guilty of adultery

> were to sit an hour on the gallows, with ropes about their necks,—be severely whipt not above 40 stripes; and forever after wear a capital A, two inches long, cut out of cloth coloured differently from their clothes, and sewed on the arms, or back parts of their garments so as always to be seen when they were about.

The situation with the crime of incest was somewhat different. In 1692 Massachusetts made it a capital offense, but in 1695 changed the sentence, as lacking conformity with the law in England. Now the penalty was the same as for adultery, except that the convicted were to wear "a capital I, two inches long of a proportionable bigness, cut in cloth of a contrary colour to their cloathes" and displayed in the province ever after. But incest, the same year, became an especially difficult issue in Massachusetts. So Samuel Sewall indicated in conscientiously borrowing from Increase Mather a little book called ". . . Whether it is Lawful for a Man to Marry his Wives own Sister?" The question was painful, Sewall noted, because "several have married their wives sisters, and the Deputies thought it hard to part them." But a vote of 27 to 24 decided that such alliances did violate the law of God. Close as the tally was, it is hard to see how the deputies could have determined otherwise. In an attempt to be as conservatively Hebraic as possible, New England Puritans defined incest Levitically, thus greatly exceeding the bounds of simple consanguinity. They greatly exceeded Leviticus itself, Chapter 20 of which their law cited, in ruling criminal a man's converse with his "grandfather's wife, wive's grandmother . . . wive's father's sister . . . son's son's wife," and other implausible couplings.

Hawthorne may have known of the act, which was on the books for nearly a hundred years, or not. What he would have known was the most dramatic entry to be found in the tome he twice withdrew from the Athenaeum, Felt's *Annals:*

> 1681, March 29. Two females, for incest, are sentenced to be imprisoned a night, whipped, or pay 5 £, and to stand or sit, during the services of the next lecture day, on a high stool, in the middle alley of Salem meeting-house, having a paper on their heads with their crime written in capital letters.

It was "probably in Felt's Annals," as Hawthorne wrote in "The Custom-House," that he remembered reading of the decease of Jonathan Pue, once like himself Surveyor of Customs for the port of Salem. It was in Pue's hand, in old ink on dingy paper, he says, that he read "a reasonably complete explanation of the whole affair" of Hester Prynne and her legendary letter. In writing his version of it, he admits to having dressed up the account as he liked. But he quickly adds that he still has the original papers, which will be "freely exhibited to whomsoever . . . may desire a sight of them." For posterity, presumably, "I contemplate depositing them with the Essex Historical Society."

That Salem institution had already merged

into the Essex Institute, still flourishing. But in pretending to give facts he had in fact invented, Hawthorne was once more—profoundly, and as he knew—concealing a deeper truth. As he could not have known, he was also predicting the final repository of old documents more memorable and significant than Hester's. It was a long-range forecast: they came officially to rest at the Essex Institute on December 10, 1980.

But it is hard to think that Hawthorne had not discovered the real papers, which related most directly to him, some time before he was himself Surveyor of Customs. From the long list of works borrowed—for him, by Ebe—from the Athenaeum, it is clear that he studied his regional past broadly and intensively during his solitary years on Herbert Street. Elizabeth Peabody remarked how he "made himself thoroughly acquainted with the ancient history of Salem." As for his family's past, deep in the town's, he had not one but two older unmarried relatives of the sort that become expert in matters genealogical. He availed himself of both. Old Eben Hathorne, as Nathaniel entered in his notebook, was a forlorn bachelor whose great hobby was "the pride of ancestry." He had "a good many old papers," and an "old book, with the record of the first emigrants (who came over 200 years ago)" in his own hand. (Presumably lost when his house burned shortly after he died.) He "kept telling stories of the family, who seem to have comprised many oddities, eccentric men and women, recluses, &c."—plus "some bastards." Eben also passed it on that "old Susy Ingersoll has a great fund of traditions about the family," which she had got from her mother, Eben's sister. A spinster recluse herself, in a dilapidated old manse one day to be known as the House of the Seven Gables, Susy did not live all alone. "The Duchess," as Nathaniel called her, made her own contribution to family and town gossip by adopting the motherless son of a man who had recently been her gardener.*

The Duchess and Eben were naturally Hawthorne specialists. But they knew well that the father of their young relative had married into a family old to Salem and grown more prominent than their own. And if they were up on family scandal along with other local lore, there was nothing to eclipse or match the one that engulfed the children of Nathaniel Hawthorne's great-great-great-grandparents, Richard and Anstice Manning. What is most likely is that they would

---

* The boy, educated at Yale, became the Reverend Horace Conolly. He inherited the house, which had by then become the setting for a well-known book, and took the name Ingersoll. In 1837 he told Hawthorne a remarkable story of two Acadians, separated on their wedding day. When the author decided it was "not in my vein," Conolly told it to Longfellow, who then wrote *Evangeline*.

have heard something of the son Nicholas, first Manning in the new world.*

To judge from the record, Nicholas was an adventurer. Born June 23, 1644, the first child of Richard Manning of Dartmouth, Devonshire, and Anstice Calley, he sailed to America at eighteen. The next year in Salem he married the widow Gray, who became first in a line of Elizabeth Mannings that reached Elizabeth Manning Hawthorne, Nathaniel's sister. The eponymous Elizabeth, who had a son but seven years younger than her new husband, promptly bore Nicholas four children, three of whom died as infants. Hawthorne did not inherit the urgency of this passion for matrimony. But he had a maternal ancestor as significant to him as the paternal William Hathorne. This was not his great-great-grandfather Thomas Manning, gunsmith of Ipswich. It was Thomas's older and more conspicuous brother Nicholas.

Nicholas was energetic, enterprising, and above all things family-minded, as might be said. A Salem gunsmith and anchor maker, his rise in the New World was rapid. Received into the

---

* It is also possible that one or more of the many Mannings of Hawthorne's own day would have known about the most unusual event in the family's American history. Hawthorne's maternal grandfather, also Richard Manning, lived in Salem until Nathaniel was eight, and *his* grandfather Thomas, aged seventeen, was in the same town at the time the family name was disgraced.

church and recognized as one of God's Elect, he was a juryman, constable, and a selectman in company with William Hathorne, next to whose land he purchased ten acres in 1668. At the outbreak of King Philip's War in 1675, he joined up and quickly rose to the rank of captain. Later he commanded the ship *Supply*, with forty men and thirteen guns, and captured the Indians who had made off from Salem harbor with thirteen boats. He was contentious and litigious as well, his name appearing frequently in the Essex County Court records, where he seems to have lost more often than not. He signed his name with a great initial *N*, and a final *g* as bold.

His father had died in England, but Nicholas left a considerable family there. By 1679 he was riding high. He was officially reprimanded for sporting a periwig, and in the spring he chartered the "pink or ship Hannah and Elizabeth," Lot Gourding, Captain, which crossed the Atlantic and returned from Dartmouth with his mother Anstice (frequently Anstis, though Anstice is how her surviving signature reads), his sisters Anstice, Margaret, and Sarah, his brothers Jacob and Thomas, and forty other souls—including a chirurgeon who presented a long bill for compounds such as Histericall Carmanitius suds.

The pink or ship did not put in at Boston until

September 14, but only the next year things had
become so difficult for the Mannings in Salem
that Nicholas left town under something of a
cloud. It was not until 1684 that he surfaced at
Sheepscot, Maine, as captain of a company that,
according to a citizen's complaint to the Gover-
nor, "Doth much Obraide & Disturbe vs." It was
apparently two years later that he married Mary,
daughter of John Mason, who was the largest
landholder of the region, having bought twelve
thousand acres from the same Robin Hood Major
Hathorne had negotiated with. Nicholas acquired
an interest in the property, and at about the same
time was awarded a judgeship as a supporter of
Sir Edmund Andros—recently appointed Gov-
ernor of the Dominion of New-England. When
protorevolutionary Bostonians overthrew Andros
in 1689, Judge Manning was arrested for complicity in his maladministration, brought to Boston, and imprisoned. Pleading his record of
service he was freed, and seems to have remained
in New England until 1697, where there is record
of him at Boston—despite the unpleasantness that
caused him to flee Salem sixteen years earlier. He
must also have returned to military life, for his
signature appears on the treaty with the Indians
reached at Pemaquid, Maine, in 1693. Long since
divorced from Elizabeth, who was awarded his
Salem acres next to Hathorne's, his house and two
shops and the orchard, he was by 1702 living

with Mary as a gunsmith on Staten Island. In 1719 he sold John Manning, his son by Elizabeth, rights to the Maine lands, and was last heard from in Long Island two years later. It is not known if he had offspring by Mary. But in 1768 one Thomas Manning, "Gent" of the province of pennsilvania," petitioned Massachusetts Bay for the quarter share of land along the Sheepscutt River in Lincoln County due him "as heir to John Mason."

It is conceivable that during his researches into Salem's past Hawthorne completely missed Nicholas Manning, though he is mentioned and indexed in the 1829 Felt's *Annals* as captain of a man of war, and more significant facts, along with other old papers—which considerable care had recently been taken to preserve—were close at hand. Conceivably he heard nothing curious of this first-arrived maternal ancestor from friendly Hathorne authorities, though all this seems unlikely. What seems impossible is that, in the early fall of 1833, he could have read without giving the matter further thought, in the same volume of Felt, that on March 29, 1681, two females were sentenced to go on display at the meeting house with the label INCEST on them.* What females? Incest with whom? There was

---

* It would surely have caught his eye that just below this entry is one that reads, "June 28th. Hon. Wm. Hathorne died lately AE 74." An obituary follows.

nothing like this anywhere else in the work. As he must also have known, there was only one place where Felt could have discovered such a bit of social history. If he did not, Felt gave it in a note: "Qt Ct.R."

New England Puritans were contentious and litigious in general. A great deal about the vicissitudes of their daily lives can be learned from the primitive account of their experiences with the law: in Salem, its "Quarterly Court Records," Felt's source. The town had a judicial tribunal as early as 1636, when the first sessions of the court of what became Essex County were held there; that is the date of its first surviving document. By 1655 it had some sort of courthouse that needed repair, which stood on what was then called School Street. About twenty years later a new house was erected in the middle of that thoroughfare; in Hawthorne's day the functioning courthouse, completed in 1786, was on the same street, now called Washington. It was a two-story brick building with a cupola on top of the roof and a balustrade on which the Father of His Country had stood. When Nathaniel was a boy, the lower floor was fireproofed for the protection of judicial papers stored there. In 1817 these documents were placed chronologically in ledgers. It was here, very likely, that Hawthorne read how on 24: 9: 1668 Judge Hathorne and others sentenced Hester Craford for fornication with John Wedg. If so, he must have read that on the same day Hester's sister Susana accused Stephen Haskett of fathering the child she murdered. These papers were readily available; in 1836 it was spelled out in print that the clerk of the courts was to maintain them "in good order, and to keep convenient and correct alphabets to the same." The handsome building of Hawthorne's youth was torn down to make way for the railroad. But a larger granite structure opened in 1841, and a brick one beside it twenty years later. It was in the newer building that the early records reposed—out in the open to be handled by anyone, unobserved—until they were prudently removed at last to the Essex Institute.

Even on a fine day, dark red brick against the blue, the joined mid-nineteenth-century museum-like buildings of this establishment on Essex Street are not so appealing as the Custom House, unless to special admirers of Victorian Italian Revival architecture. But unlike the Custom House this is a busy, thriving institution with large holdings and many treasures—among them the author's desk when he was Surveyor at Salem, and the Charles Osgood portrait of him at thirty-six, every bit as handsome as Elizabeth Peabody said. To examine the recently acquired Records and Files of the Quarterly Courts of Essex

County, Massachusetts, the contemporary in-
vestigator enters the Institute and turns right on
the ground floor into Daland House, which contains the James Duncan Phillips Library. It is a
large, airy, pleasant room. He pays two dollars
for a yellow card. Close-mouthed, he ignores
the nine openly shelved volumes of the court
records to 1686: they abstract and print the old
documents, he means to see the originals again.
Having searched them when they were stored in
the brick courthouse where they rested for 120
years, he knows what he wants to copy. He asks
the attendant at the reference desk for ledger
number 35. She disappears into an area marked
"Staff Only," and heads for the fireproof section
of the library, where specific items are shelved
in locations the Institute does not disclose.
Against the walls all around him are works of
genealogy and town or county history. She returns with the ledger, which she takes to the
table where he is sitting. He remembers from
years back that what he is looking for is fixed to
page 69.

And so Hawthorne, on some kind of day of
some unknown year, must have walked over to
Washington Street, and entered the attractive
courthouse of his time in search of records he
would never so long as he lived forget. His feelings cannot be known—or, perhaps, even plau-

sibly imagined. But the facts are pretty clear. On the first floor were the great ledgers registering some two hundred years of provincial tribulation. After leafing their pages for a while, watching the passing dates, he would eventually have come upon the events of March 29, 1681, which Felt reported. In the middle of page 69 in the thirty-fifth ledger was pasted a piece of old rag paper, of good quality in very good condition—not much stained or "foxed," not "dingy" but lightly tinged yellow. In ink somewhat brownish but very clear, a strong hand that he could make out almost entirely had written, three hundred years ago now:

> Anstis Manning & Margaret Manning now Polfery being brought before the Court at Salem in November 1680 for incestuous carriage with their brother Nicholas Manning who is fled or out of the way, & bound over to this Court at Ipswich March the 29: 81 for farther heareing[.] The delinquents appeared & the evidences being read & considered. This Court doth sentence the said Anstis & Margaret to be comitted to prison untill morning & then to be whipt upon the Naked body at Ipswich, & that the next Lecture day at Salem then shall stand or sitt upon an high stoole during the whole time of the Exercise in the open middle

ally of the meeting house wth a papper
upon each of their heads, written in Capital Letters This is for whorish carriage
wth my naturall Brother. And the Constable of Salem is hereby ordered & en-
joyned to see that it be performed as to
show so appeareing at Salem as above
said.*

If he did not know it already, Hawthorne
would quickly have learned that the delinquents
were the English-born offspring of his direct
ancestors. If he read on in the record, and looked
a little back, he would have learned more. First
he would see that on September 30, 1680, complaint was made against the two women "for
lewd carriages wth theire Bro . . . as lying together in y[e] same bed severall times the particulars
of which carriage will farther appear by y[e] Evidences given in to this Court"; they "stand
charged with viz: Vehemenent suspicion of com-
mitting incest." Just over two months later,
Hilliard Veren, clerk of the court,** entered in

---

* Immediately beneath this entry on the same piece of paper, a
smaller, more difficult hand in different ink has noted that in
answer to a petition the court grants that by "paying 5 li
[livres (pounds)] in mony shall be remitted ¼ part of the
sentence by whipping . . . the other part . . . to be executed
att Salem[.]"
** Veren, or Verin, was officially clerk from 1658 to 1683, when
he died. Conceivably Hawthorne encountered the fact that
for the same quarter century he was also collector of customs
at Salem.

his distinctive, slightly crabbed hand the first of some striking and specific "Evidences." It was that of Elizabeth Watters, servant and eye-witness, who

> testifieth that sum time the last winter . . . att night there was a quarreilling & disturbance between my master Nicholas manning and his wife whereupon his wife went away out of the house & Lodged att another place & In that very night . . . being a thirst . . . [she] passed thorrough the Roome whear her master and his wife used to Lodge Together & . . . I heard a womans voice which I judged to be Anstis Maning In the bed I heard her say who Is that softly I heard my masters voice In the same bed Answer softly be quiet[.] Then this examinant went up . . . to my felow servants ann kelegrew and grace Stiver . . . and tould them . . . upon which we all agreed to Rise Early in the morning to see if we should find them In bed together which we did . . . & we passed thorough the Roome Into the kitchings & left the dore for open that we might see what they further did & . . . saw the offor said Anstis Manning arise out of the bed without her clothes except only an under petticote which we conceived she had then sliped on & presently I saw my master . . . arise out of the same bed without his clothes . . . and put on his

clothes siteing by the bed side. . . . Anstis
. . . came Into the kitching & s^d to us . . .
are you up already[?] This Examinant
further testifieth that she hath severall
times since seene her master Afforesaid In
bed under the bed clothes with the said
Anstice . . . and Like wise his sister
margarett . . . severall times [and] that
the s^d nicholas came Into the Room where
this examinant was Alone & put his hand
under her coats and kist her & attempted
to throe her upon the bed but she crieing
out he did forbear further actions[.] She
further testifieth that the morning above
mentioned . . . An Kelegrew called her to
Look on the bed when she made it & she
saw the bed much stained of a Red
colour[.]

Sworne in court at Salem . . .

On the same date, Ann Kelegrew and Grace
Stiver (both passengers with the Manning sisters
on the *Hannah and Elizabeth*) testified to "the
truth of all the above written that Related to
theire sight" of both Anstice and Margaret—
particularly to "a Red Couler wherewith the
bed was much stained." Ann added that her
master "hath severall times tempted her to lie
with him saying to her Lett me. If I be with Thee
an hundred times I will not get thee with child."
Two of Manning's daughters-in-law swore on
the same date that they feared being alone with

the captain, "and Elizabeth saith that one time using some unsivill cariage towards her made her afraid he intended some further eveil [and she] Said to him these words (how can I doe this & sin against God) Where upon he flung awaye very Angry."

Preserved in the court record is the humble petition (in a clerk's hand, but signed E.m.) of Elizabeth Manning, the aggrieved wife, stating that for about half a year, frightened of her husband and his two sisters, and without means, she had lived with one of her daughters. Nor, she went on, did he wish her to return—until the night before the accusations against him were made. Then in her simplicity, as she says, she was overcome with his fair speeches and went back to him, only to find "his intent was to make use of me butt as a cloake (alas I know so much of him & his sisters y^t hath been a terror to me)." Next Elin Maskoll swore that Mrs. Manning had told her of having several times seen "very wanton cariages betweene her husband manning & his sisters as kissing & tumbling on the bed together" but was afraid to speak. There is also the humbler petition, in her own hand, of the widowed mother of the guilty siblings. It is a large sheet, badly torn, with pieces missing and a good deal that survives indecipherable, but some of its spirit remains:

... into the part of ye Earth ... Affliction
... desolation ... my own family ...
fatherless Children ... my daughters had
committed this heinous ... I should certainly be dum with ... almost constantly
in my Company ever since this cuntry
... that my son nicholas ... I hope y^e
Lord will change his hart & ... merciful
to ye widow and Strangers as I and my
Children are in this land ... little ... am
capable of

Anstice Manning

Son Nicholas was long fled. His sisters and
Margaret's husband petitioned for remission of
the fine "which yor honors have Legally sentenced us to"—adding, in an apparent admission
of guilt, "the Justice wher of we must
acknowlege." (Another section of the record
shows that a fine was paid.) Then in 1683 Elizabeth Manning was "freed & released from hir
marriage," it having convinced the Court of
Assistants of the Colony of Massachusetts Bay,
"on perusal of the paper's presented," that her
husband was guilty as charged, and declared he
would not have "any thing to doe" with his wife.
What the record does not show, though there is
a reference to her "present condition," is that by
the time she was officially on display at the meeting house Margaret Manning Palfrey was seven
months with child. The question of paternity was

inevitable. There is no known answer to it; a few of her descendants were prominent citizens. She was twenty-four. Her sister Anstice was already thirty, but eventually married a middle-aged widower named Powling. Relatives kept alive for a while her unusual given name. Thomas Manning, Hawthorne's great-great-grandfather, christened his first daughter Anstice.

So tired and contrived seems the whole business of a terrible family secret, recorded in a hidden old document, its very staleness has helped prevent even the suspicion that there might be something alive in it. So extraordinary, then— yet credible and tragic—the actual transcript, that the attempt to find a fictional fascimile for it, which a protagonist contemporary with Hawthorne could somehow be cursed or influenced by, was obviously doomed. But at the end of his career, determined to practice his trade when he had lost the gift of it, Hawthorne clung to materials that were in his vein, even though it was occluded. Having exhausted his paternal ghosts, and laid them to rest, he turned to guiltier, more troubling maternal ones that he could not think how to use.

Not that he had kept them completely out of his work before then, though here much depends on what cannot be definitely established: the time he first learned the Manning secret. According to Ebe, she read what was then called "Alice Doane" in the summer of 1825. If at that early date her brother (and perhaps she) knew the story of Nicholas, Anstice, and Margaret—which was enacted in the same place and period as the story of Leonard, Alice, and Walter—it seems sure that his most unusual tale is a reworking of crucial bits of family history, as suspected with less reason before. Indeed the Manning paradigm would help account for what might otherwise seem redundant, or supererogatory, in his fiction: the incestuous triangle. A single relationship in violation of this taboo is ordinarily dramatic enough to go it alone, having no need for the rivalry that animates a standard three-sided affair. Perhaps the precedent explains the recurrence of the pattern. The recurrent name Alice for the young man's sister may also trace to the Manning disaster: Hawthorne could not come any closer to Anstice, which was not particularly serviceable.* He would, then, have taken both Alice and her triangle from the old scandal, simply and plausibly reversing the genders to one sister, two brothers. If, on the other hand, as is quite possible, Hawthorne uncovered the historical facts after having written "Alice

---

* Neither Alice Pyncheon of the *Seven Gables* or Alice Vane of "Edward Randolph's Portrait" has an incestuous role or overtones. But they do share with Anstice the fact that it is as strangers newly from abroad that they play their dramatic parts in early Massachusetts.

Doane," the discovery must have proved an even
greater shock. In addition to having come upon
a piece of unforgettable bad news from home,
as it were, it must have seemed as if he had somehow "forecast" the past—or had all unaware
been so in its grip that he had virtually repeated
it, at least in fiction. Either way, the facts were
indelible, and came near emerging at the end.
Less bluntly and less effectively, he reworked
the Alice Doane arrangement of sexes in the
"Footstep." Following that, he returned to the
original one; Septimius Felton has two "sisters,"
one dark, one fair, and he experiences erotic
sensations with both, as did Nicholas Manning.
It is as if the whole "Oedipal tendency" of Hawthorne's fiction had been proclaimed by a
Quarterly Court at Salem.

The same court papers also confirm the suspicion raised in the cases of both Felton and
Middleton that the guilt of a "first American
ancestor" had nothing to do with any Hathorne.
A specific and different immigrant is evoked at
least once. When Sybil tells Septimius the legend
of the bloody footprint, he thinks sharply of
"long ago," and "the first known ancestor of his
own family, the man with wizard attributes, with
the bloody footstep . . . whose sudden disappearance became a myth." The presence, or de-
parture, of "brother Nicholas Manning who is
fled" is immediate. Indeed it begins to look as

though the Ancestral Footstep of Hawthorne's last works was in his mind everywhere implanted by Nicholas—who never in the fiction disappeared without leaving the permanent mark of his crime, the nature of which is finally plain. So the hale and manly blacksmiths in the fiction—notably Danforth and Hollingsworth—must have been associated in Hawthorne's mind with Mannings, who were metalworkers from Nicholas down to Nathaniel's grandfather Manning.

Far more to the point, however, is the realization that the testimony of the Manning maidservants to the forbidden behavior of their master with his sisters—and the indelible, homely, scarlet evidence of it they adduced—make transcendently clear that for the author the bloody footprint was the very symbol and sign of Nicholas, the mark of his consanguine guilt. To carry the matter to the heart of things, Hawthorne regularly associated, or even equated, blood and guilt. It has already been argued that his essential vision of the world, diabolically revealed to him as young Goodman Brown, was "to behold the whole earth one stain of guilt, one mighty bloodspot." Now it appears that the dutiful servants uncovered the source not only of that distinctive imagery but of the vision itself, Hawthorne's apocalypse. The sentence of the Quarterly Court made the dreadful truth final and formal, but with the prior testimony the dye was cast.

Such observations are not made casually, but they relate in the end to an even more serious matter that cannot be avoided. Since Hawthorne's ancestral secret turns out to be of a piece with Clarel's startling insight into Vine's, and since he admitted to having inherited "strong traits" from forebears that are not to be found in those he draws attention to, but might be in the ancestors he kept hidden, and since the ultimate secret of dark ladies is said to be of the same nature, there does not appear to be any way around the question of the relationship between Nathaniel and Elizabeth Hawthorne. The least that must reluctantly be suggested, and the most that can be responsibly intimated, is that it looks as if Something Happened. Just what that may have been—and the range of possibility is broad —it would be as fruitless as vulgar to guess. A very conservative position could call on the argument of "Fancy's Show Box." It could have been something inward, nothing overt. Guilt can arise from deeds which, physically, "never had existence." All alone in a "midnight chamber . . . the soul can pollute itself"*—with the "ghosts

---

* *Self-pollution* was commonly conveyed by the term in Hawthorne's time. *Webster's Third New International Dictionary* still gives "emission of semen at other times than in coition" as a definition of *pollution*.

of . . . never perpetrated sins." It would follow that the guilty female shades, which elsewhere haunt that chamber, were all in the mind of Oberon. The lustful heart has sinned already, as the Gospel according to Saint Matthew announced.

Guilty thoughts, however, are common to practically everyone, and the deep blue region of Hawthorne's guilt seems peculiarly his. It stretches credulity to think that his nature contained such an area of culpability as a result of nothing more than imagination or longing. Nor does it seem likely that something other than self-knowledge gave him the idea that "moral diseases which lead to crime" are passed down the generations—or that he was thinking of an infirmity not connected with the earliest Mannings. Hawthorne felt himself freed, or rescued, or saved by marriage, but in his last work seems returned to his dungeon—the darkest corner of it. Perhaps he felt that if he could master in fiction what once again bothered him it would cease to do so. "If he wrote it he could get rid of it" is a thought that has found its way into Bartlett's *Familiar Quotations.* So in the past Hawthorne had exorcised matters that appear to have troubled him: boyhood submission, in a couple of early tales, to his Uncle Robert; phantom visitors to his solitary room; even, perhaps, by way of a flashback in "Alice Doane's Appeal," the guilt-charged shock of his father's sudden death. Surely the vivid specters of compromised females in the Show Box of Fancy, in Dimmesdale's private quarters, as well as in the Haunted Chamber, reflect something that had burdened him—which in some way had "happened."

But where Hawthorne came closest to dealing with the weight he would most like to get rid of, "secretly confessing" his own secret, as it were, and where he came very near doing what he said he could not do—lead the sympathetic mortal across the veiled abyss of his nature and into his depths—is in *The Scarlet Letter.* Failure to hear his confession has resulted from his own success: first in putting readers in mind of the wrong ancestors in "The Custom-House," and then of the wrong symbol throughout the romance. The clearest account of Hawthorne's un-told tale is the buried story of the minister and Hester.

It had seemed improbable that Hawthorne could have conveyed so eloquently the force of Place in Hester's life—how a dark event that colored it rooted her to the region of its occurrence—without having experienced at Salem something of the kind himself, or without knowing of any shame that attached to his deep roots there. Knowing these hidden roots, and of the

crime that clung to them, remarkably increases
a reader's sense of the immediacy of the author's
relation to his book. This is striking on Hester's
first appearance—in "The Market-Place," where
"her sentence bore, that she should stand a certain time" and did, "fully revealed before the
crowd" to show her letter under the weight of
a thousand eyes. Impossible, in visualizing this
scene, that Hawthorne could have erased from
his mind the image of Anstice and Margaret
standing, or sitting upon a high stool,* before the
congregation during the whole time of the exer-
cise at the meeting house, wearing letters grimmer
than Hester's. Perhaps they thought wistfully, as
she does, back to their native village in Old
England, and their "paternal home . . . of antique
gentility." Very likely it was of them he thought
first, then of Hester. But it is doubtful, as he
pictured things, that they wore on their heads
the wordy indictment the court dictated. On
their breasts, rather, the capital *I* two inches long
of a color contrasting to their clothing that the
law would very soon prescribe for Salem. And
as Hester stood with her infant in her arms before
the staring women—uppermost in whose minds
was the "riddle" of its paternity—Hawthorne

---

* Originally the "stool of repentance" placed in Scottish
churches for the display of offenders, especially against
chastity.

must have been aware of the darker riddle that pressed on those who stared at Margaret "Polfery" and her imminent expectation. The guilty Dimmesdale, who is fled for the time, will hide an *A* on his chest until he confesses it and dies; it is unlikely that Nicholas Manning felt any need to confess the invisible *I* he took to the grave. But more than once the breasts of the author's afflicted heroes were lacerated with guilt, and in this book, in his own way, the author will confess it.

His way is partly through establishing recognizable relationships to the characters in it. In a limited but real sense, he is represented as Arthur Dimmesdale, author of powerful sermons, the chief literary genre of his time and place—in the line of Oberon, another writer and another guilty witness of female ghosts. As for Dimmesdale's daughter, all who have read Hawthorne's descriptions of his child Una as a youngster have recognized Pearl's origins in his life. Una was born in Concord to "The New Adam and Eve"; Pearl was "worthy to have been brought forth in Eden." But the marked resemblance of Hester Prynne to Elizabeth Hawthorne—another dark lady, eventually rejected—seems to have gone quite unnoticed.

It adds up. Both women were distinctive for independence of mind and spirit. Both were intellectually and morally bold. As Ebe was "a good deal unspiritual," indeed "unregenerate," Hester is so uninterested in the spiritual and religious matters that are life itself to her lover it is a wonder that the author does not remark or account for the fact. She tries to persuade her minister that they should simply sail off into the broad world from their narrow province. Her sin has effectively ostracized her, but she does not even believe in it. "What we did," she pointedly tells Dimmesdale, "had a consecration of its own." (This romantic position so frightened the author of it he is quick to remark that Shame, Despair, and Solitude "had made her strong, but taught her much amiss.") Both women were dark, isolated beauties, knowing little of the world but not innocents; both were "sensible," strong, unafraid, decisive, frank, shock-proof. In defiantly embroidering her *A*, Hester is even "rather perverse." Aside from accidental motherhood, needlework is her only sign of domesticity, as knitting was Ebe's. Both women are "at home outdoors"—Hester in chapters called "A Forest Walk," ". . . at the Brook-Side," and "A Flood of Sunshine," where the "whole richness of her beauty came back." She is the only really effective dark lady in Hawthorne. Like Ebe, she is "excellent," and possessed of loving-kindness. And by the time Hawthorne wrote his book, Ebe was in a retirement more secluded than Hester's even after Pearl was grown and gone, Dimmesdale and Chillingworth dead.

Chillingworth, the husband, is not of this family—but essential to a related one. A misshapen, diabolical figure with an evil eye, he is roughly equivalent to the wizard who was responsible for the incest in "Alice Doane's Appeal"—and not unconnected to that "first ancestor" with "wizard attributes" who echoed Nicholas Manning. This is to say that like the wizard in the early tale, Chillingworth in *The Scarlet Letter* takes responsibility for the sexual transgression that ruined everyone but Pearl, the product of it. A man "already in decay," he admits to Hester, it was his folly in marrying a young and beautiful woman that led straight to her "blazing letter." Thus in a special but very real way, Dimmesdale is Hawthorne, Hester stands for his sister, and Pearl is his daughter. Chillingworth represents the controlling force of "witchcraft"—which, as Hawthorne told Longfellow, had made him captive in the dungeon of his own chamber (where his Fame, and maybe his Infamy, was won).

But in that "blazing" letter there is a serious problem. And the solution to it solves whatever mysteries are left in "The Custom-House."

Despite its power and penetration and durability, there is a weakness at the heart of *The Scarlet Letter*. It is the awkward disproportion between the reality of adultery and the unreal horror with which it is regarded in the book. Puritans took adultery seriously, and punished it in several ways—severely. Yet in Hawthorne's romance they do not react to it as to a sin against the sanctity and vows of marriage, but as something more obnoxious, repulsive. It is somewhat as if, turning to life, Hester Craford's crime, which was fornication, was as revolting as her sister Susana's when she killed her child. Hawthorne's view is as extreme as the community's, and he becomes increasingly insistent on it. As noted before, he claimed that his book was "positively hell-fired" without ever explaining how. So, apparently, was the *A* itself; long after Hester he put it on his own breast and felt its "burning heat"—his own experience of sensations several tortured characters had suffered in that region. So superstitious townspeople claimed Hester's letter was "red-hot with infernal fire." It does indeed appear that something about his symbol was eluding his grasp, and some deep meaning to his story escaping with it.

The hellfire burns in the missing elements. In this case, at least, D. H. Lawrence was absolutely right: if he is to get to the heart of the matter the reader must look through the surface, and discover "the inner diabolism of the secret meaning" of *The Scarlet Letter*. It far evaded Lawrence, but nothing Hawthorne wrote makes the point as firmly. He saw through the surface of his symbol well enough, and no aspect of it got past him. It is readers who fail to see, since he covered it over so thoroughly, that in Hawthorne's mind Hester's *A* is an *I*. His book really deals, as he said it did, with "the taint of deepest sin in the most sacred quality of human life." Adultery cannot compete for that title.

What is actually going on becomes clearer and clearer as the story approaches its end, by which time the *A* is completely unsuited to the way people view it. In "The Procession" which leads to the close, a "rude and boorish" crowd acts out the point. It thronged about Hester, and then "stood, fixed . . . by the centrifugal force of the repugnance which the mystic symbol inspired." If the symbol is an *A*, as the reader has been relentlessly reminded, it is absurd now to call it mystic. It is equally unreasonable to think that the letter could immobilize with repulsion an assembly of country folk—or city. And then, underlining this implausibility, Dimmesdale speaks out to destroy completely the *A*'s credibility. He takes the occasion of his farewell address to "People of New England!" to redirect their attention to the object that has already transfixed them. "It hath cast a lurid gleam," he cries, "of awe and horrible repugnance" about Hester. "Ye have all shuddered at it!" The same mark has been on his breast, he confesses, and the devil—once more the familiar image— "fretted it continually with the touch of his burning finger." And finally, as if this were not already more than enough, at his death hour, Dimmesdale incredibly

> "bids you look again at Hester's scarlet
> letter . . . with all its mysterious horror."

The only thing mysterious about the *A* is why he and the New Englanders found it revolting. As if in a desperate last charade, author and minister are straining frantically to make the people see what diabolical letter—sin, crime— lies just beneath the surface.

It has not worked. People have not understood. But when in "Conclusion" Hawthorne points a single moral from his tragic tale, he feels he has done all he could. And the message is remarkably applicable to him:

> Be true! Be true! Be true! Show freely to
> the world, if not your worst, yet some
> trait whereby the worst may be inferred!

He was probably satisfied that this is what he had himself just done. The "trait" he mentions is an "essential" one, such as he invited readers to look for in fictitious characters like Dimmesdale; it is a "strong trait" of his ancestors, such as he said had intertwined with his own nature. And now from it, perhaps, the "worst" has been inferred. When he broke down in trying to read the newly finished ending of his book to Sophia, he must have felt that at last he had been true, though she did not understand either. Having stood with Dimmesdale—having become Dimmesdale, struggling to publish his letter before he died— he had got it off his chest. It might also be that there was an obscure family relation between the emotional upheaval in reading the passage to his wife and the one that attended the death of his mother.

With Dimmesdale, Hester, Pearl, and Chillingworth the principals on stage at the finale, and the crowd behind them become a chorus, in voices of "awe and wonder," the last scene of *The Scarlet Letter* brings to a climax the book's remarkably operatic quality. All eyes are on Dimmesdale in his redemptive agony. But as much as Hawthorne had invested in the minister, he was very likely conscious too of another figure standing obscure and motionless in the wings. This would be the dim, improbable, hulking presence of Samuel Johnson, transported ghostlike from Uttoxeter, where in eloquent silence he had like Hawthorne expressed his guilt. Hawthorne was powerfully drawn to the tale, which he told three times, of how Samuel Johnson, having once refused to tend his sick father's bookstall in the marketplace of that town, returned to it fifty years later to stand, bareheaded in the rain for an hour, where it had stood. On his fifty-first birthday Hawthorne recorded in his notebook his "pilgrimage" to that "holy site." He searched there for the right location, which is unrecorded. Presumably he wanted to stand a moment himself.

Penance, too, is good for the soul. On finishing his book, Hawthorne thought he might feel better. Having thrown, he says, all the light he can on the letter imprinted in Dimmesdale's flesh, he hopes to "erase its deep print out of [his] own brain," where "long meditation has fixed it in very undesirable distinctness." Having written it, he hoped to get rid of it; he had dealt with many things by writing them. And then, in the last line of the book, he invokes yet once more the appearance of an *A*, still glowing red in the gloom. But this does not mean he had failed to exorcise the image that had become oppressive. For that was of an *I*—worn and bleached, very likely, until it had faded white. So, fulfilling his name, may Oberon have blanched on first exposure to the old record that spelled the letter out.

Now in his own way, so far as he was able, Hawthorne had spelled it out in his romance. And still kept "the inmost Me behind its veil," as he announced he would do in "The Custom-House." Under the triple cover of persona, symbol, and substitute ancestry, he had confessed his secret and kept it too.

Reprise:

Domestic Resolutions

THE notebooks Hawthorne kept in this country between 1835 and 1853 run to something like two hundred thousand words. They were his blend of diary and commonplace book, in which he made notes on his travels, on characters encountered, walks enjoyed, reading, random thoughts or bits of information, and so forth. In particular he made suggestions to himself, usually without precisely dating them, concerning matters he might do something with in a tale or sketch. When he actually pursued and realized one of these, as happened very occasionally, readers seize on the instance in pleasurable recognition. "A snake taken into a man's stomach," for example, "and nourished there . . . tormenting him most horribly. A type of envy or some other evil passion." Or, "A person to be the death of his beloved in trying to raise her to more than mortal perfection."

Very little attention has been paid to suggestions that have potential relevance to the writer instead of his work. An example of this can be found after the date of December 6, 1837, where he wrote, "A dread secret to be communicated to several people of various characters,—grave or gay,—and they all to become insane, according to their characters, by the influence of the secret." Another item of conceivable significance to Hawthorne the man appears under the date of October 24 of the next year. "Each circumstance of the career of an apparently successful man to be a penance and torture to him, on account of some fundamental error in early life."

As the context makes clear, the thought of Samuel Johnson at Uttoxeter prompted the second entry. The reader may be prompted in turn to wonder if Hawthorne was perhaps picturing himself having achieved the fame and success Fanshawe-Oberon dreamed of, and Johnson won, only to find the rewards excruciating— as would Dimmesdale—in the realization of radical unworthiness, born of an ineradicable sin in the past. It is even more natural to wonder if the notion of a terrible secret becoming known to various people who go mad of it grew out of his discovery of the original Manning disgrace. In any case he did record, in the same series of ideas that lists the one about the baleful secret, a thought that clearly related to his own professional struggle and long-range ambitions: "A man will undergo great toil and hardship for ends that must be many years distant,—as wealth or fame, —but none for an end that may be close at hand." It was not the first time he had entered this sort of observation. Late in the previous summer he noted that "what we need for our happiness is often close at hand, if we but knew how to seek for it." As the recently discovered manuscript of this notebook shows, he drew an X through the paragraph in which that sentence appears—probably when he wrote, during the winter of 1837, a modest tale which purports to embody that not especially original theme.

"The Threefold Destiny" (1838), subtitled "A Faery Legend," presents Ralph Cranfield as far-traveled, and dark-skinned from his journeys. But beneath the thin veneer he is still Fanshawe, another young man with a vision of "undying fame," marked out for a "high destiny." He is convinced, either through witchcraft or a prophetic dream, that three marvelous things are in store for him. One is the love of a beautiful woman, who will be known by an emblem on her breast in the form of a jewel shaped like a heart. Another is discovery of a place, revealed to him alone, where a mighty treasure is hidden in the earth. Last he will gain great influence and power.

Having vainly wandered the world in search

of these boons, Cranfield returns to the house of his mother. Here, in his "well remembered chamber," he passes a "wilder night than ever in an Arab tent, or . . . haunted forest." A "shadowy maid," not altogether unexpected by the reader, steals to his bedside and lays her finger on his "scintillating heart." A flaming hand points to a mystery in the ground. A wand beckons the dreamer toward a chair of state. Such are his nocturnal fantasies.

In light of day they look somewhat different. The "visionary Maid" who visited his bed is Faith Egerton, "playmate of his childhood." Here where he left her, now with a jeweled heart on her bosom, is the fated love of his life. Their faces glow with "kindred feeling, flashing up anew from half-extinguished embers." Then the hero learns that to find the mysterious treasure he is to "till the earth around his mother's dwelling, and reap its profits!" Last he discovers that the mighty office in store for him is that of instructor in the village school. The legend ends with a complacent moral:

> Would all, who cherish such wild wishes, but look around them, they would oftenest find their sphere of duty, or prosperity, and happiness, within those precincts, and in that station where Providence itself has cast their lot. Happy

those who read the riddle without a
weary world-search, or a lifetime spent
in vain!

Doubtless Elizabeth Hawthorne applauded.
And apparently the reader is supposed to feel that
although Ralph might have spared himself a lot
of travel he is at least fortunate in discovering,
while he can still enjoy it, his destiny in the
everyday norm. Or one might conceive that the
author, confronted with himself as a middle-aged
bachelor still stationed in the spot he occupied
as a boy, was wishfully or resignedly picturing
a domestic resolution to his long frustrations.
Perhaps he was in the right place after all?

If, as suggested, Ralph's was a "dream of prophecy," a kind of unwitting sense can be made—
for the writer behind Ralph's mask—of that
contented thought. Buried in the earth about
Hawthorne's native home, as he early suspected
and had begun demonstrating, was the rich lode
of the regional past, which he would mine at
such great profit. Nothing in the soil of Brook
Farm or the dust of Rome would turn up treasure comparable to what he realized from digging
in the history of his own area. As for influence
and power, it has been precisely in the schools
of the land where Hawthorne has wielded his
widest sway, if scarcely over children.

A few have looked backward instead of forward from this tale, and read it as Hawthorne's minor version of *Rasselas, Prince of Abyssinia* (1759), a didactic romance by the venerable Samuel Johnson. Johnson's young prince—wearying of existence in a pleasant valley of the Nile, and believing that "happiness is some where to be found"—seeks to fulfill himself through experience of the great world beyond the mountains. After various adventures, having failed to find what he was looking for, he returns home. Thus ends the similarity to Hawthorne's story. If Cranfield has found prosperity and fulfillment in the place of his birth, as Hawthorne's moral suggests, what Rasselas has discovered is the sober truth—and this is Johnson's moral—that "human life is every where a state in which much is to be endured, and little to be enjoyed." It is a fact that Johnson wrote his book in a week's evenings to pay for his mother's funeral. But his judgment was the product of a mature and tempered intellect, not of temporary affliction. Hawthorne, on the other hand, had yet as an adult to leave home. His legend passed judgment on a life he hadn't lived, drawing a conclusion he hadn't reached.

He would, however, himself observe in a Preface to his *Snow-Image*, 1851, that

> In youth men are apt to write more wisely than they really know or feel; and

the remainder of life may be not idly spent in realizing and convincing themselves of the wisdom which they uttered long ago.

Conceivably so, and in Hawthorne's case. When he wrote his tale of Destiny, some of his best fiction was almost a decade behind him. But it is true as well that even as he wrote it, in the early winter of 1837–1838, and published it in March, he was in the process of leaving the precinct and station where Providence has cast his lot. No longer obscure, his *Twice-Told Tales* had appeared a year before, and Longfellow's glowing notice in the *North American Review* had announced him to the world. He had recently met and fallen in love with Sophia Peabody. Then, on January 4, 1839, he learned that he could have an inspectorship in the Boston Custom House. The railroad from Salem had opened the previous summer, and within two weeks he was on his way, permanently terminating the long seclusion in the house of his mother.

And so in the context of the author's own story, the tale seems an odd sort of hail and farewell to a protracted youth. The suspicion grows that he was either unthinking and unconvincing, or ironic. Whatever the legend's explicit moral, it is not plausible that Cranfield, descendant of Fanshawe and Oberon in his confidence of a great destiny, would be content harvesting his mother's half acre when free of his schoolchildren. On the matter of his great love, the reader of Hawthorne as a whole has special misgivings. It is all so familiar: the "visionary" female who steals to the bedside of a too-well-remembered chamber, wilder than a haunted forest, and lays a finger on his burning breast. Whatever the meaning of her symbol or emblem, she remains the sisterly shade, grown playmate of childhood, glowing like her beloved with "kindred feeling," which flashes from coals ignited somewhere in the past. Maybe, like the tale of Alice Doane, the young man's dream really was induced by witchcraft. In any case, in its pat and simplified resolution it self-destructs.

Only that heart-shaped jewel at the heroine's bosom, which marked her for the hero's heart's destiny, is left dangling. What is perfectly irrelevant to the tale, but may say something about its author, is that almost immediately beneath the second of the two entries in the American notebooks which anticipate "The Threefold Destiny," Hawthorne imagined

> An ornament to be worn about the person of a lady,—as a jewelled heart. After many years, it happens to be broken or unscrewed, and a poisonous odor comes out.

So much for the heroine's emblem. She was, after all, out of a fairy tale. What leads deeper into Hawthorne's nature, finally, than any dream of destiny is part of the last entry in the American notebooks, made just before he left for England in 1853. "What a trustful guardian of secret matters fire is!" he writes. He has just burned, as he records, "hundreds of Sophia's maiden letters"—all of them. But a letter of his own survives to preserve the substance of one of hers, which he might particularly have wished to suppress.

Fourteen years earlier, shortly after he departed Salem for Boston and began the long courtship by mail of Sophia, she wrote him about a "disturbing dream" in which she had received a letter from him addressing her as "My dear Sister." James Mellow, who came upon his response in the Huntington Library, remarks that "knowing the value of dreams," Hawthorne "immediately sensed . . . some holding back" on Sophia's part. Whatever it was he sensed, he was clearly disturbed himself. "I wish you had read that dream-letter through," he told her, exactly as if it had existed. "I am very sure it could not have been written by me. . . . Mine own Dove, you are to blame," he argues a little sharply, "for dreaming such letters . . . as coming from me. It was you that wrote it—not I."

In Mellow's opinion, he was "overreacting." Sophia, it will be remembered, said she never had a glimpse behind the veil he drew around him. But Hawthorne knew the potential danger of dreams. "The mind is in a sad state," he later remarked in "The Birthmark," "when Sleep, the all-involving, cannot confine her spectres within the dim region of her sway, but suffers them to break forth, affrighting this actual life with secrets that perchance belong to a deeper one."

Acknowledgments
and Afterthoughts

A SHORT book can spend a long time in the back of one's mind. It was during the 1964 centennial of Hawthorne's death that I announced in a talk (published the next spring in *The Kenyon Review* and reprinted in my *Three Bags Full: Essays in American Fiction,* 1972) that I thought I knew his secret. I wasn't ready to reveal it, however, and for one reason or another four books intervened before I got to this one. Some of my notions about the writer obviously go back further than that. I had begun reading him more or less in earnest back before World War II, partly because of an association with Austin Warren, whose American Writers Series *Hawthorne* (1934) was already venerable. Specific ideas also trace quite a way into the past. In particular I remember reading an essay by Hyatt Waggoner on "Alice Doane's Appeal" not long after it appeared in the summer of 1950 (*University of Kansas City Review*). I had never read the tale itself, and the critic scarcely touched

on its powerful sexual charge. I was taken, nevertheless, with his impression that there was some
"tremendously significant revelation of Hawthorne here," and when I searched out the story
I had a similar feeling. Notes I took at the time
unaccountably survive, and I see that though I
knew little then about Hawthorne's life and
family, I sensed somehow his deep involvement
in the piece. That was probably the beginning
of this book.

It was at about the same time that as a random
reader of nineteenth-century American fiction
I here and there encountered the figure of the
dark lady, to whom I had been introduced by
D. H. Lawrence. I knew a little about Elizabeth
Hawthorne from Randall Stewart's then standard
biography of her brother, but had no special
interest in her until I came across Robert Cant-
well's fuller account of her in his biography
(1948). At least a decade elapsed before I encountered the striking portrait in her niece Rose
Hawthorne Lathrop's *Memories of Hawthorne*
(1897). Then I was more forcibly struck with
Ebe's resemblance to the dark lady, whom I had
gotten to know better betimes. (She was fully
introduced to American fiction in Charles Brockden Brown's *Arthur Mervyn* [1800], which I
wrote about in *The Southern Review* [Summer
1981].)

Off and on, over this extended period, my sense of the sexual element in Hawthorne quickened. Blindness to it in some of his scholars is monumental, but I have learned a bit from those with better vision—Leslie Fiedler for one, who also stems from D. H. Lawrence. But the situation here is confusing. I have read and reread Fiedler on Hawthorne, chiefly in *Love and Death in the American Novel,* and can no longer distinguish what I first perceived through him from what I discovered for myself. Where I might seem to owe him most, indeed, I think the debt is not real, each of us having arrived at much the same conclusion independently and by different routes. I am thinking of *The Scarlet Letter,* which Fiedler calls, as in effect I do, "a work about guilt written out of guilt." He then says, taking a great step in the right direction, that in his book the author "may be dealing, half-consciously at least, with the sin of incest"— which has been "translated down" to a lesser crime. Except that I think Hawthorne knew exactly what he was dealing with, I can't improve on that.

But it is by a spectacular intuitive leap that Fiedler has reached this position. He does not explain what it is based on, or show how incest enters the novel in any way or at all—except that he knows of the Manning scandal, and thinks the sisters were sentenced to wear the letter *l*, instead of the wordy inscription that was actually prescribed. I suspect that my sense of Samuel Johnson's presence at the book's concluding scene was picked up long ago from Mr. Fiedler's. But though he is good on the dark lady in general, we do not much overlap in the case of Hester Prynne, and our views of her origins in life are widely separated. Fiedler thinks there was indeed a real-life "model" for all Hawthorne's dark ladies: she was the "tall, darkeyed, queenly maiden who rejected" the author when he apparently proposed marriage in 1836. This is a leap that lands nowhere. Not even the woman's name is given, and nothing whatever is known of her except that Randall Stewart, from whom her brief description is silently taken, identified her as Eliza Gibbs of Edgartown, Martha's Vineyard—and gave as *his* source an "unpublished reminiscence." There is no good reason for supposing Hawthorne proposed marriage to any such person; "maiden" is a curious term for a dark lady—who in any event does not reject suitors, it being her destiny to be rejected.

Another partial anticipation of this volume is Frederick C. Crews's *The Sins of the Fathers: Hawthorne's Psychological Themes* (1966). When I first heard about this work I had a feeling my book had been written for me. That turned out to be not at all the case, though Crews certainly has pieces of it. He sees the lovers/ siblings relationships clearly, and how Hawthorne was oppressed by his sense of ancestry, and how ancestry related to incestry. Like Fiedler, he knows of the ancestral Manning disgrace but makes nothing whatever of it. Fair enough; he is not interested in Hawthorne personally, or in his life, only his work; he mentions Elizabeth Hawthorne once in a footnote.*

A work that does make something of the Manning past did not surface for me until I was well into writing this one. It is an unpublished Princeton dissertation called "The Paradox of

---

* A likeness of Elizabeth as a live Dark Lady of Salem was a consummation devoutly to be wished. But a long watch had availed none, and it began to seem more and more likely that she never submitted to a portrait, nor saw any reason to. Expert Hawthornians do not know the location of any picture—or else remember a photograph which turns out to be that of Elizabeth Peabody, Nathaniel's sister-in-law. The search did not, however, end with completion of this book. In response to my subsequent inquiry, Rita Gollin, who assembled all known *Portraits of Nathaniel Hawthorne* in a volume (1983), suggested that there might have been Ebe related items, if no picture, in a Hawthorne exhibit mounted in 1904 at the Essex Institute on the centennial of his birth. Back to the library, where I eventually discovered that the January, 1905, issue of *Essex Institute Historical Collections* published a complete inventory of this display. Under Portraits and Photographs there are twin surprises:
Elizabeth Hawthorne, sister of Nathaniel Hawthorne. Tintype, bust. *Loaned by Mrs. Richard C. Manning*
Elizabeth Hawthorne. Tintype, bust, with a lock of her hair, in a frame. *Loaned by the Misses Philbrick*
No one appears to know what happened to these pictures. Today the Essex Institute has neither of them. According to its

Benevolence: Hawthorne and the Mannings"
(1977) by Gloria Erlich. She clearly perceives
"covert autobiography" in the fiction, and the
presence of Manning history. She treats Elizabeth
Hawthorne candidly, so far as she goes; she relates the author's "Alice" to "Anstice" and to
Hester's *A* but not to his sister.

Modern knowledge of the Manning scandal,
where it uncommonly exists, stems entirely from
a passage in an admirable but little-read book by
Vernon Loggins called *The Hawthornes* (1951),
which I learned of a decade late. The Manning
part of it attracted virtually no attention on
publication and has been put to very little use,
but with it things began falling into place for
me. And I was startled to discover, much more
recently, that the remarkable facts Loggins publicized had been in print since 1921, when the
Essex Institute published them. For the source of

Reference Librarian, Hawthorne artifacts were purchased from
the estate of Richard Manning when he died, but nothing is
known of either tintype. The only individual I could find with
a personal recollection of having seen the picture, long ago, is
Manning Hawthorne, whom I met some thirty years back in
Bangalore. Mr. Hawthorne reports that he has a "dim memory"
of Richard showing him such a picture—which he imagines is
at the Essex. No descendants of Richard Manning are known.
Rebecca, last Manning to occupy the Herbert Street home-
stead, has long since died, and her mementos did not include
the missing photograph. The house was sold into private hands.
But the Institute does have a pane of glass from a window of its
haunted chamber under the eaves, on which a young man
entering his anonymous apprenticeship etched "Nathaniel
Hathorne, Salem, March 30th, 1826" with a diamond.

his facts and quotations, the author gave in his notes *Records and Files of the Quarterly Courts of Essex County*. Since no date was attached, as with other books, I thought the reference was to the documents themselves, from which he certainly appeared to be quoting. These I itched to see for myself, though it was not until August of 1977 that my wife, Katherine, and I made our way to Salem, found the old brick courthouse where they rested at the time, on open shelves in great ledgers, and before long came to the original papers, which survived in the absence of formal security. Belatedly it dawned on me that Loggins's source was not these ancient documents at all, but Volume 8 of the published tomes, which bear the title he gave (adding *Massachusetts*). He also fails to mention the fact, noted in the introduction to the first of these volumes, that the records had *not*, in these compilations, been transcribed verbatim, but "in abstracted form, free from needless verbiage." Since the few who have cited the bare facts of the Manning disaster have relied exclusively on Loggins, no one who has mentioned his study in print had seen and described or transcribed the original documents —or known, since he did not, of critical ones that were overlooked.

The long period during which some of this information remained undisseminated is also remarkable. The fact that Nicholas Manning, by name, was "guilty of incestuous practises with his sisters" was published in 1901, when the official papers of the Court of Assistants of the Massachusetts Bay Colony, which recorded his wife Elizabeth's divorce from him, were printed in Boston. (Her right to "what estate can be found . . . for her maintenance and support" was entered in records published there in 1854.) Given the considerable and long-lived interest in both Hawthorne and—because of the witch trials—late-seventeenth-century Salem, it is simply unaccountable that the "two females, for incest"—spotlighted by Joseph Felt in 1829— were not for 120-odd years identified and related to the author.

Just as curious, in a different way, is the avoidance or suppression of the Mannings' dark history and its implications for Hawthorne by his most recent, exhaustively informed, and otherwise responsible biographers. It is not a matter of ignorance. The late Arlin Turner, in *Nathaniel Hawthorne: A Biography*, and James R. Mellow, in *Nathaniel Hawthorne in His Times* (both 1980), not only knew about Loggins's work, they used it. Turner cites it twice in the notes to his first chapter, where he makes a good deal of the Manning role in Nathaniel's youth, but is completely silent on the family's past. Mellow gives Loggins as a source but then, ignoring him, states that the Mannings could trace their lineage back to 1679, when they "arrived in America." This is to erase from the record Nicholas, who brought over his mother and siblings at that time, having already become, during seventeen years here, a prominent citizen and soldier of Salem.

A completely different sort of afterthought to the present study, offered in passing, concerns the matter of parallels between Hawthorne and William Faulkner. These are numerous and occasionally bemusing—such as the shared preoccupation with incest, little remarked, where at points the lines run so close they nearly touch. The thought, for example, of Hawthorne searching an old court ledger and coming on the crude facts about the shamed Mannings is uncannily akin to the memory of young Ike McCaslin in a crucial passage of *Go Down, Moses,* where he learns from a primitive entry in another old ledger—of the family plantation—that his grandfather begot a son on his daughter by his Negro mistress, who drowned herself in response (*"23 Jun 1833 Who in hell ever heard of a niger drowning him self"*). Even more remarkably, the plot of "Alice Doane's Appeal" foreshadows *Absalom, Absalom!* where again at the crux of the action a brother kills a brother—again called a "deeper, darker self"—who is aiming to commit incest with their sister. (Confronted, once, with a lesser parallel, Faulkner asked, "Who's Hawthorne?")

A delayed answer to another question concerns the nature of the "secret sin" of Walpole's *Mysterious Mother* mentioned in the epigraph to Chapter 1 here. It is the same curse that afflicted the Mannings and McCaslins. Walpole's "untold tale"—which, incidentally, deeply impressed Melville—was that of a widowed lady who discovered that her son had an assignation with one of their servants. To expose him in this lawless passion, she arranged to take the damsel's place, only to keep her identity secret when she was overcome by her own lust. A daughter was born of this union, and raised privately in the country, the son having been sent away. But the daughter, grown to lovely young womanhood, met the son by accident. In all innocence they fell in love and married. Thus the girl's husband was her brother and father as well. Walpole said he heard this when young as a true story from an archbishop, but it was already an old and more than twice-told tale.

*　　*　　*

A short book can pile up a much longer list of debts than yet mentioned, or could if one had record or recollection of so much as half of them. I owe my facts about Hawthorne, and some of what I hope is my understanding of him, to a number of his biographers, beginning with the earliest and coming down to now. As for his work, I have over a period of some thirty-five years read, or read in, or looked into dozens of books that deal with it, and hundreds of articles (including unpublished ones from a long line of graduate students). Again the question of to whom I owe what, if I owe it, is in many cases hard to answer. Most points I touch on have been handled, in one way or another, by many others. I alone, however, am responsible for the central notion about the nature of Hawthorne's secret.

Debts of other sorts are entirely clear. For vetting the entire job as it progressed in typescript I am grateful to my wife Katherine, my stepson Stanton B. Garner, Jr., and my colleagues Wilma R. Ebbitt, Robert N. Hudspeth, and Robert A. Secor. They are all good readers, and resonant sounding boards.

So is Richard E. Winslow III, friend, historian, and demon researcher. As in my last excursion (*Revolutionary Ladies*, 1977) he joined up voluntarily and selflessly, and made himself invaluable. He furnished me with William H. Manning's overlooked *Manning Families of New England* (1902), which documents much of what we know about Nicholas (while remaining ignorant, apparently, of the reason for his leaving Salem permanently and for his subsequent divorce). He turned up relevant data on late-seventeenth-century developments in sexual crime and punishment, such as a good account of the instituting of the 1695 Massachusetts "Act to Prevent Incestuous Marriages," in *The Diary of Samuel Sewall* (1, 333), M. H. Thomas, ed. (1973). Also the texts of the 1692 and 1695 incest laws from *The Acts and Resolves, Public and Private, of the Province of Massachusetts Bay* (1, 208ff, 1869); *The Law of Adultery and Ignominious Punishments* by Andrew McFarland Davis (1895); and the formidable *History of Matrimonial Institutions*, 3 volumes, by George Elliott Howard (1904). (According to this work, the earliest case of a woman sentenced to wear the single capital *A* occurred in March of 1707 at Plymouth, Massachusetts, where one Hannah Parker was condemned to be set on the gallows, receive thirty stripes on the naked back, and wear ever after the capital *A* [2, 175]. "Singularly enough, her paramour was acquitted"—and, "she being big with child," her punishment was suspended for the time being.)*

---

* Agreeable to the possibility of ancestral overlap with Hawthorne, whether through witchcraft or adultery, I seize on Hannah Parker's name and place of residence. My maternal great-great-great-great-great-great-grandfather was Deacon Thomas Parker (1605–1683), who came to Lynn, Massachusetts,

Dick Winslow performed a couple of services of such value to me and this book that I thought he ought to appear in it, albeit incognito: he, in fact, is the nameless sleuth who visited the Essex Institute on my behalf to check out the notes I made on the Manning records in the old court-house six years ago. Actually, he had already found them out for me when first I told him I had learned, so I thought, from Loggins of their existence. He made sure they were available and accessible. But when I got to them, and began deciphering and copying, I realized that a lot of painstaking work needed doing in a chaotic setting and bad light, as he had warned. On the same day, however, I was assured that through the proper agency, which can go unspecified, I would have no trouble procuring excellent photographs of any pages I needed. I decided to

in 1635, moving to Reading four years later. He had two grand-sons, Samuel and John Parker, who took wives named Hannah, who would have been of child-bearing age in 1707. (Lilly Eaton, *Genealogical History of the Town of Reading, Massachusetts* [1874].) Deacon Parker had eleven children by his wife, Amy, one of whom was Mary Parker, born in 1647. A woman by that name was executed for witchcraft in Salem on September 22, 1692, before the magistrate John Hathorne—along with one Alice Parker and the better-known Martha Cory, referred to in "Young Goodman Brown" as "that unhanged witch." (These were the last witches put to death in New England.) According to a book of my mother's cousin Jean Clarke Caldwell, we are descendants of Martha Carrier, also remembered in "Young Goodman Brown" as—here Hawthorne quotes Cotton Mather—"the hag whom the devil promised to make the Queen of Hell." Salem, Plymouth, and Reading were not far apart. .

do that, whereupon repeated efforts and protracted delays availed but a single useful picture
(of the tattered testament of Anstice Manning,
mother).

Obviously another trip was necessary, but Mr.
Winslow, who lives much nearer Salem than I
and had business there anyway, made it before
I could. He went to the old courthouse, learned
that the records had been relocated, and succeeded at the Essex Institute in obtaining a clear
reproduction of the essential document—the
sentence—here given for the first time in full.
And that junket led to a joint, last, and telling
discovery.

The long periods during which the facts, let
alone the text, of the Manning scandal were never
published, and the additional decades that elapsed
before Loggins related them to Hawthorne, have
been remarked. Add to this finally the fact that
the evidence that convinced the court of the
guilt of the accused has never seen the light of
print until now. As reported in the *Records and
Files of the Quarterly Courts* (8, 88), all testimony is reduced to a note that "abstracts" it
(without needless verbiage) to the point where
it is impossible to know what the evidence was,
or even to tell if it was cogent. It is recorded of
Elizabeth Watters, servant, only that she "testified to the relation between said Manning and his

sisters." And of Ann Kelegrew and Grace Stiver that they "deposed." Except for a little from the complaint of Manning's wife, here cited, and the claim that he had been "uncivil" to her daughters, there is nothing more. In ignorance of the witnesses and their depositions, therefore, Loggins could hold out the possibility that the whole matter of incest lay, as he puts it, in the "unbalanced mentality" of Manning's "frenzied wife"—who, clearly, was frightened not frenzied, destitute not unbalanced.

Loggins was unaware that the evidence still exists because he did not go to the documents themselves but to the published *Records and Files,* the compilers of which thought the testimony unnecessary—or more likely, in 1921—unfit to print. Going to the documents, however, I originally missed it too: the testimony was submitted three months before the sentence was pronounced, and so appears seventeen long, hard to read, and irrelevant pages before the punishment is spelled out. Between us, Winslow and I did not come on it until the very end. *Potius sero quam numquam,* as Livy said. Better late than never.

Thanks, then, are extended to the Essex Institute for making available all the old documents now deposited there—particularly to Irene R. Norton, Reference Librarian, Caroline Preston, who has charge of manuscripts, and Marylou Birchmore, who handles photography. Even as this was written, the Massachusetts State Archives had begun removing the court papers from the ledgers, restoring them, filing them in acid-free folders and boxes. And so will be enhanced the longevity of a few documents—along with a great store of other records—without which Hawthorne was a somewhat different writer, different man. One thinks warmly as well of the long line of anonymous souls who watched over these papers in their previous repositories. And does not forget, come to think of it, generations of such indifference that not even worms did try the long-preserved virginity of the record. (Nor its dishonor turn to dust. Or into ashes all its lust.)

INDEX

Index

HAWTHORNE'S SECRET was set by Maryland Linotype, Baltimore, Maryland, on the Linotype in Janson, a recutting made directly from type cast from matrices long thought to have been made by the Dutchman Anton Janson, who was a practicing type founder in Leipzig during the years 1668–1687. However, it has been conclusively demonstrated that these types are actually the work of Nicholas Kis (1650–1702), a Hungarian, who most probably learned his trade from the master Dutch type founder Dirk Voskens. The type is an excellent example of the influential and sturdy Dutch types that prevailed in England up to the time William Caslon developed his own incomparable designs from them.

The book was printed and bound by The Maple-Vail Manufacturing Group, Binghamton, New York. The paper was S.D. Warren's #66 Antique, an entirely acid-free paper.

Typography and jacket design by Dede Cummings.
Jacket calligraphy by George Laws.